PRAISE FOR
EFFECTIVE SALES MARKETING

"Aligning sales and marketing strategies is a core part of my role internally at my company but also consulting with our clients. It's hard to get started and never fully solved but this book offers great insights on how marketing can better support sales so companies can start improving alignment today." **Mike Weir, Senior Director, Sales, LinkedIn Marketing Solutions**

"From the C suite to the fulfilment team, the impact of generating more sales will affect the entire corporation. Tapping into the knowledge of the marketing team and having that team work, not side by side, but integrated with the sales team, is genius. *Effective Sales Enablement* is a growth generator." **Ginger Shimp, Senior Marketing Director, SAP**

"This book is going to help you move from 'sales trends' to 'business solutions'. The actions, insights and advice Pam shares in this book are valuable to everyone driving revenue for their organization. If you want to move from theory to implementation, *Effective Sales Enablement* is the best tool to impact your business. This an engaging book with actionable insights and a delightful perspective made possible thanks to Pam's enterprise-level B2B experience." **Mark Godley, CEO, LeadGenius**

"Marketers cannot be successful without a strong understanding of sales. *Effective Sales Enablement* will help align marketing and sales using effective sales enablement tools. Pam Didner draws on her decades of experience to show how this melding of marketing and sales teams is a win–win for companies, customers, and overall business. A must-read." **Nancy Bhagat, CMO, Communications Solutions Segment, TE Connectivity**

"Internal silos are the biggest threat to creating a customer-centric organization. And the biggest one I've seen to date is the gap between sales and marketing organizations. Didner's *Effective Sales Enablement* is PURE GOLD. It provides a marketer's perspective on how to increase the business impact of any sales organization. Highly recommended to marketing and sales leaders alike!" **Ekaterina Walter, digital transformation leader, international speaker, author of *The Laws of Brand Storytelling***

"Is Sales from Mars and Marketing from Venus? Better, how much more success would you have if all the planets were aligned? Pam makes complete sense of the sales and marketing universe in this book. Read this. Then get your teams to read it." **Robert Rose, Chief Strategy Officer, The Content Advisory**

"Most sales enablement books are about sales training and development. It's refreshing to find a sales enablement book written from a marketer's point of view. Didner shows how you can integrate your marketing elements into external sales efforts or vice versa. A must-read for sales people and marketers." **Alana Zamora, Senior Director, Global Content Marketing & Strategy, Medallia**

"This book will help any business create a sales enablement plan that will grab the attention of everyone up and down the corporate ladder." **Emma Hitzke, Global Head of Marketing, Intel Artificial Intelligence**

"With this book Pam Didner draws on her decades of experience to show how the melding of marketing and sales teams is a win–win for companies, customers and overall business. Her real-world examples give great guidance on how to excel in your role, whether that is marketing or sales." **Jeff McKittrick, Senior Director of Digital Sales Platforms, Cisco**

"Look no further. We finally have a hands-on masterplan for bridging the often-adversarial marketing and sales relationship. Sales and marketing alignment is much discussed, but rarely achieved. *Effective Sales Enablement* is the playbook for realizing that goal." **Pawan Deshpande, CEO, Curata**

"The most useful and specific guide ever created for B2B marketers to shepherd sales success. 100% recommended!" **Jay Baer, founder of Convince & Convert and co-author of *Talk Triggers***

Effective Sales Enablement

Achieve sales growth through collaborative sales and marketing

Pam Didner

KoganPage

Publisher's note

Every possible effort has been made to ensure that the information contained in this book is accurate at the time of going to press, and the publishers and authors cannot accept responsibility for any errors or omissions, however caused. No responsibility for loss or damage occasioned to any person acting, or refraining from action, as a result of the material in this publication can be accepted by the editor, the publisher or the author.

First published in Great Britain and the United States in 2019 by Kogan Page Limited

2nd Floor, 45 Gee Street	c/o Martin P Hill Consulting	4737/23 Ansari Road
London	122 W 27th Street	Daryaganj
EC1V 3RS	New York, NY 10001	New Delhi 110002
United Kingdom	USA	India

© Pam Didner 2019

ISBN   978 0 7494 8364 7
E-ISBN   978 0 7494 8365 4

British Library Cataloguing-in-Publication Data

A CIP record for this book is available from the British Library.

Library of Congress Cataloging-in-Publication Data
Names: Didner, Pam, author.
Title: Effective sales enablement : achieve sales growth through
   collaborative sales and marketing / Pam Didner.
Description: London ; New York : Kogan Page, 2018.
Identifiers: LCCN 2018024737 (print) | LCCN 2018029115 (ebook) | ISBN
   9780749483654 (ebook) | ISBN 9780749483647
Subjects: LCSH: Sales management. | Marketing.
Classification: LCC HF5438.4 (ebook) | LCC HF5438.4 .D53 2018 (print) | DDC
   658.8/1–dc23
LC record available at
https://catalog.loc.gov/vwebv/search?searchCode=LCCN&searchArg=2018024737&searchType=
1&permalink=y

Typeset by Integra Software Services, Pondicherry
Print production managed by Jellyfish
Printed and bound in Great Britain by CPI Group (UK) Ltd, Croydon CR0 4YY

*To the unsung heroes who work behind the scenes
to enable their sales teams.
Keep moving forward. You rock!*

CONTENTS

ABOUT THE AUTHOR

Pam Didner is a content marketing leader, author and speaker. Having held various positions at Intel, she led many of Intel's enterprise product launches and worldwide marketing campaigns. Her position supporting direct and indirect sales teams as a marketer has given her a unique perspective for sales enablement with expertise in delivering global marketing and sales success.

Her first international book, *Global Content Marketing*, offered an accessible, comprehensive process to scale content across regions. She was selected as one of BtoB's Top Digital Marketers in 2011 and 2012. *Global Content Marketing* was named one of the top 10 marketing books of 2014 by Inc.

Pam has been a repeat presenter at highly regarded conferences such as Content Marketing World, Social Media Strategies Summit, Media Hungary, Integrated Marketing Summit and more. She has given presentations in the US, Asia, Europe and Central and South America. She was an adjunct instructor at West Virginia University and the University of Oregon School of Journalism. She is an expert at creating successful global marketing plans that meet the needs of local marketing and sales teams. She leads a boutique consulting firm that trains, coaches and provides strategic guidance on audience development, messaging architecture, editorial planning, content creation, and sales and marketing collaboration on a global scale. Her clients include Intel, 3M, Sunstar, Cisco and TE Connectivity, to name just a few. She also shares marketing thoughts at her site pamdidner.com and contributes articles to the *Guardian*, the *Huffington Post*, Content Marketing Institute and elsewhere.

PREFACE

Misfortune is a blessing in disguise

For some, it's a stigma to work for one corporation for almost twenty years. For me, it was a blessing. I know. I know. It's not cool and considered old school to stay at a company for that long. But I was fortunate to join a wonderful company that encouraged its employees to change positions and departments to enable a deeper understanding of the overall organization while avoiding stagnation. I started in finance and accounting, then moved to project management, product support, procurement, supply-chain management, marketing operations, event marketing, sales support and global marketing strategy and planning. I was also blessed to learn first-hand how a global enterprise operates through a wide array of positions.

This diversified experience also taught me to see the same event through different internal stakeholders' eyes. When I was searching for buy-in, I was able to speak their language. For example: when I made a pitch for marketing budget to the sales team, I emphasized marketing campaigns that focused on the bottom of the purchase funnel. When I talked to finance, I honed in on budget updates and return on investment (ROI). When I spoke to product marketing teams, I shared value propositions and product content that we promoted through integrated demand generation campaigns. I've learned through my experience that the story I tell needs to be about them, not about marketing.

Technology makes it both easy and challenging to support sales

The mentality of 'it's all about them' served me well when I worked with both direct and indirect sales teams. It was not easy supporting them, but it was one of the most fabulous and frustrating experiences of my career. I supported sales when digital marketing started to flourish, and social media was on the cusp of blossoming. I recognized that lines between sales and marketing were becoming blurry. At certain points, we were stepping on each other's toes or were in conflict with each other due to different departmental goals. New technologies made us productive separately, but it didn't bring us together, since the tools we used were not integrated. Using separate tools also created duplications and inefficiencies. A perfect example: email marketing, traditionally, was marketing's job. But salespeople can easily run their own email marketing campaigns using features in sales enablement or customer relationship management (CRM) tools. Unless these two tools talk to each other and the teams coordinate, we might not provide a seamless user experience and can lack a holistic view of analytics on email performance.

But new technologies also offer marketers additional capabilities to elevate marketing programmes and identify potential sales enablement opportunities. The digital component of partner marketing, affiliate marketing and loyalty programmes can be integrated as part of a sales enablement marketing effort. For example: marketers can design banner ad space in a mobile app in keeping with the user experience while showcasing a key account's product. Another example: while marketers produce their own 'how-to' content, they can also showcase customer content to demonstrate how those products can also solve their target audiences' challenges. Sales teams need to understand how to leverage technology and their customers' content to create win–win marketing scenarios.

Bring marketing to sales enablement

Conventionally, marketing's role in sales enablement has been:

- drive demand generation
- work closely with sales on nurturing prospects
- fulfil content needs
- aid sales training and onboarding
- craft value propositions

As boundaries between different functions evolve and merge, marketing's role will need to expand to:

- identify marketing elements that can be part of the sales discussion
- educate sales in key marketing programmes
- help sales teams understand technology's impact on marketing and sales
- brainstorm specific marketing programmes that can aid sales negotiations
- integrate sales and marketing tools

This book provides insights and ideas on how to better align with sales from the perspective of marketers. This requires brainstorming, planning, and collaboration. At the same time, it also requires marketing to be nimble and spontaneous. Planning and collaboration are indispensable, but you'll need to adjust marketing tactics and budget allocation when salespeople need help closing deals.

Who should read this book

This book is targeted at business-to-business (B2B) marketing professionals who are interested in supporting sales or who work closely with the sales team. Sales professionals, sales operations managers and sales enablement managers can also benefit by understanding what marketing can do to further enable and support sales.

Intended audiences:

- marketing agencies and consultants who work closely with sales teams
- B2B sales and marketers in enterprises as well as growing start-ups
- Millennials and entrepreneurs who decide to start businesses and want to know how to integrate sales and marketing
- any company interested in refining and implementing sales operations and enablement

What this book is

This book will give you strategies and knowledge to implement and improve your sales enablement strategies, processes and programmes. After finishing this book, you will:

- understand trends that impact sales professionals and how to take advantage of them
- become a better marketer with creative ideas on how to support sales
- be able to integrate sales elements into select marketing programmes
- comprehend technology's impact on sales enablement
- gain insights on how to assemble a first-class sales enablement team

What this book is not

In an ever-changing world, no single book can provide exact steps that will apply to every situation. After incorporating the philosophies and tactics you learn in this book, you will need to extrapolate and modify the ideas and processes, so they work for your companies and your clients.

Sales enablement is a broad field. Below is a list of topics that are touched upon in this book, but they are not focus areas:

- sales onboarding process and methodology
- training development and creation
- sales incentives and compensation structure
- sales operations organizational structures
- sales processes and methodology
- customers' purchase journey

A quick chapter overview before you start

There are some day-to-day and immediate sales enablement challenges: sales reps spend up to 43 hours per month searching for information they need. More than 90 per cent of content goes unused by sales teams. Eighty-seven per cent of sales training skills are lost within a month.[1] Friction occurs between sales and marketing. Lack of productive sales tools or even too many tools to use overwhelms sales teams. Every company's sales enablement challenges are different. By talking to many marketing, sales ops and sales enablement managers, I've come to realize that every company 'enables' their sales differently. There is no one-size-fits-all answer. I don't attempt to boil the ocean and address all the issues. I would like to share how some companies deal with the issues.

Chapter 1 explains my observation of sales enablement evolution from Leonardo da Vinci to the information age. It will give you a holistic perspective on how technology evolution impacts the development of sales enablement.

Chapter 2 touches on future trends that will impact sales professionals and marketing. Trends help you see the forest from the trees and identify future initiatives to better support your sales team.

Chapter 3 discusses marketing roles in sales enablement and suggestions to address friction between sales and marketing. I also reiterate the importance of joint priorities, lead definitions and service level agreements.

Chapter 4 explains how brand, branding and messaging framework apply to sales and sales enablement. Essentially, the sales team is the frontline interface of a brand. Marketing creates the brand guide, but it's up to employees to bring brand promises to life.

Chapter 5 illustrates sales training and development. I share examples from different companies about training, sales content and coaching. Interesting enough, these elements also help account-based marketing in some ways.

Chapter 6 details how salespeople can leverage marketing programmes and use them as talking points or even as bargaining chip during sales negotiations.

Chapter 7 explores design and user experience in the context of sales engagements and processes by focusing on interactive content into sales processes and training, sourcing user-friendly tools and creating intuitive and buyer-focused marketing communications.

Chapter 8 proposes the elements you need to establish a sales enablement team. I present the key questions that you should ask and the steps that you can take to build a team. The team structure closely follows what you want to accomplish.

Chapter 9 is about technology. To share the technology's role in sales enablement, I cover three areas: tool selections for different stages of the sales process, big data analytics and the usage of artificial intelligence. It's a brave new world.

Chapter 10 is about action, action, action. Everything you read in this book sounds good, but it does not mean anything unless you take action. Robert Frost's poem 'A Servant to Servants' pretty much sums it up:

> He says the best way out is always through.
> And I can agree to that, or in so far
> As that I can see no way out but through...

Hopefully, there are some nuggets that you will find useful in this book. Just remember, when marketing is done right, sales and marketing can coexist beautifully.

But wait. There's more...

I have included case studies and recommendations that will help you apply the strategies and techniques discussed in the book to the real world. In addition, I've provided guiding questions at the end of each chapter to help you identify specific actions you can apply to your company or situation.

It's time to dive in and have fun

You can jump around between chapters. You won't get lost. Feel free to tweet or post your thoughts about this book on Amazon, LinkedIn, Facebook, Twitter, or your blog. You can reach me at www. pamdidner.com or @ PamDidner. Let's continue the sales enablement journey together.

#SalesEnablement rock on.

Note

1 Content Raven. Incredible easy sales enablement tips to close more deals. Infographic. http://raven.contentraven.com/hubfs/sales-enablement-infographic.pdf

ACKNOWLEDGEMENTS

When I was little, I was sick so often that my mother was worried that I wouldn't live very long. She took me to see a fortune teller and asked if I would survive my childhood. The fortune teller told her that, not only would I live to a ripe old age, but I would also travel to many strange places and, eventually, move to and live in a far-away place thousands of miles from my hometown. Her little girl leaving her and moving away? In my mother's mind and experience, only men moved away to explore new opportunities; women just didn't do that. The fortune teller was speaking rubbish. My mom chose only to believe that I would live long and ignored whatever he said about travelling and leaving home.

When I grew older, I got sick less and became a normal and healthy child. I eventually left Taipei, Taiwan, studied abroad, got married to a wonderful man and ended up living in Portland, Oregon (far, far away from Taiwan). My global roles at Intel took me to many countries. When I left Intel, I thought I'd travel less and instead work on client projects remotely. Who knew that my first book, *Global Content Marketing*, would take me to twelve countries in three years and allow me to get acquainted with many marketing professionals around the world, both in person and online?

As I travelled and talked to many talented and knowledgeable marketers and salespeople, it became evident to me that marketing is a behind-the-scenes sales force, and that sales is another marketing channel. I had specific points of view, an outline and some knowledge but was not sure that I had enough insights to write a 70,000-word book. So, armed with my ideas, I talked to many professionals in sales enablement, marketing, sales operations and sales management. Their insights along with my research and experience shaped the development of the book.

Stephen Sklarew connected me with many sales enablement professionals. Paul Krajewski offered insights about the inception of sales enablement. Nancy Bhagat, a long-time mentor, reminded me that marketers need to have a solid go-to marketing plan before engaging with sales. My immense gratitude to Alana Zamora for collaborating on the marketer's dilemma chapter and sharing her sales enablement experience.

I was able to get different perspectives from my interviews with Lara Sibley, Myk Pono, Tamara Schenk, John Barrows, Kimberly Miracle, Chuck Steinhauser, Diane Walker, Boyd Davis, Verne Lindner and Mark Godley. Bob Meindl made sure that I covered the indirect sales side of sales enablement. Emma Hitzke discussed how silos divided sales and marketing and shared possible remedies. Pawan Deshpande, William Wickey, Lee Levitt, Amy Pence, Iris Chan, Ginger Shimp and Ken Chizinsky shared their valuable hands-on experience and expanded the scope of sales enablement beyond just sales training and development. I also want to thank Tom Martin, Daniel Burstein, Ed Brice, Nicolas de Kouchkovsky and Sanjit Singh for letting me use their images and case studies.

Karen Straka, my beloved designer, worked tirelessly with me to create illustrations for each chapter. She turned around over 30 images in one week. I believe that I almost killed her, metaphorically speaking. Thank you, Karen. Elaine Ma, Michael King, John Trembley, and Sandy Didner were gracious enough to read the work-in-process manuscript and provided thoughtful insights and feedback.

Lastly, I want to say a big 'thank you' to my fantastic husband, Michael Didner. He not only had to put up with a cranky and stressed wife, but also edited every single chapter twice. That poor man. I couldn't do what I do without his unwavering support. It's hard to find one person who really gets you. How blessed am I to find 'the one'. Thank you for letting me be me. I love you very much, Mike!

I am a firm believer that marketing's job is to enable sales. But I am also very aware of the tension that can exist between sales and marketing managers. Sales enablement is hard, because every company has its own processes and tools for working together (or lack of processes and tools). I hope this book provides helpful insights for sales and marketing managers alike to smooth their path and create a more productive collaboration.

I can't tell you whether or not the fortune-teller could actually see my future but travelling is indeed in my blood. I love experiencing foreign cultures and learning about different people. My travel to the Château du Clos Lucé, Leonardo da Vinci's last residence, somehow inspired the creation of this book (more in Chapter 1). I am writing this acknowledgement on the Isle of Skye as the wind outside my room is howling – exactly how I imagined the Hebrides would be. Sitting in this comfortable bed and breakfast, I am thinking about how grateful I am to be able to share my thoughts about marketing at different conferences and client events, while also travelling to places that I want to visit on my bucket list. I hope that this book will continue to take me to many places. I can't wait.

Introduction

Sales enablement from a marketer's perspective

It is not necessary to do extraordinary things to get extraordinary results.
WARREN BUFFETT

As a marketing professional, successfully supporting sales takes tact, experience, perseverance, conviction and imagination. This is a lesson I learned early in my corporate career at Intel during my first encounter with sales. In one of my various marketing roles I worked very closely with the sales team, even though I reported to the marketing group. Since I was part of neither sales operations nor the sales solutions team, I asked my manager at that time what was expected of me in this role. He said succinctly: 'Enable sales to do their jobs, but don't do their jobs for them.' I remember laughing when he said that. How could I do sales' job? I was not even a salesperson.

Enable sales as a marketer

It turns out the scope of a salesperson's job can be very broad: from inside sales to outside sales, from lead research, needs analysis, responses to requests for proposals (RFPs), down to customer services and billings. Salespeople have to cover a lot of ground, but they can't do it all. Because of that, it sometimes wasn't clear where the dividing line was between what the sales team that I supported would work on and what the support team would be tasked with. My manager was smart and experienced. He didn't define the specifics of how I should support and assist my internal customers. He knew that selling technologies is hard, the purchase cycle is long and there are many moving parts. I needed to stay close to my sales team and understand their ever-changing needs, find ways to solve their issues and get them the information they needed to close sales. His advice was also spot-on, because there really isn't a dividing line between what I should do to facilitate salespeople and what they should do themselves to engage with prospects and customers directly throughout the sales process.

Here are two great examples: among my many responsibilities, I was tasked with crafting product-focused or solution-based messaging and creating content for the sales team. Since I was responsible for sales content, some sales managers started requesting customized sales presentations and pitches for meetings with their customers. From their perspectives, sales pitches were similar to content creation. It seemed like a reasonable request to them, but was that my job? Another example: we decided to create a big co-marketing campaign with one key account. I was asked to work on a co-marketing campaign plan and to present it on behalf of my sales team. Should that presentation be a joint task between sales and me? How did I respond to these two situations? In the first case, I politely pointed out that creating customized presentations was their job, not mine. But I would provide relevant slides that I believed they would need. For the second example, I gladly took on full ownership of the co-marketing plan and presented it on behalf of my sales team to the customer. I saw this as part of the marketing scope.

Yet, when I was talking to Sasha, a marketing manager supporting sales in a start-up, she told me that she took on creating all content that her sales team needed, including customized sales pitch presentations. She believed that was part of enabling her sales reps, so they could focus on selling. She was not wrong. Her sales team was five people, while mine was over fifty. There was no way that I could support customized individual presentations for all of my sales reps. Even though our jobs were similar, our responsibilities were different.

While writing this book, I had conversations with many sales and marketing professionals, marketing managers, sales enablement managers, sales operations managers, training managers and even product marketing managers. They were all enabling sales and yet, as expected, they all have different definitions of sales enablement that tie back to what they do. As former SiriusDecisions analyst Jim Ninivaggi wrote in a 2013 blog post, 'Unlike established corporate functions like accounting, finance and marketing, sales enablement is still evolving, and the term means different things to different companies.'[1] That quote still holds true today. With people, process and technologies constantly changing, the function of sales enablement will most likely continue to morph for some time.

The origin of sales enablement

The origin of 'solution selling' is well documented. Frank Watts laid claim to the term as early as 1975 at Wang Laboratories and started a series of solutions selling workshops in the early 1980s.[2] The origination of the term 'sales enablement', on the other hand, has very little documentation, with no definitive identification of who officially coined the term or when it was first used.

Cory Bray and Hilmon Sorey, authors of *The Sales Enablement Playbook*, wrote: 'As far back as 2008, articles were published about the concept of sales enablement and the necessity for sales support in B2B sales organizations.'[3] That is confirmed in a blog written by Forrester, which highlighted the discussion and outcomes of the first Sales Enablement Executive Roundtable.[4] I had several conversations with Paul Krajewski (Twitter @salesenablement), who has been tracking sales enablement progress and vendors since 2007. He has some internal documents from Nortel and BizSphere showing the term 'sales enablement' was used in 2007. He remembered several ex-IBM executives mentioned the term in 2005 and 2006, but we couldn't track them down to validate. Guess what? We turned to Google for answers, and it showed that the term was used back in 2004. Although there is no creditable document that I could find on who actually coined the term, we are at least certain the term was used around 2004.

Let's define sales enablement for the sake of this book

Even though sales enablement is situational and evolving, it's still important to define sales enablement in the context of this book.

A little bit of research will show you that there are multiple sales enablement definitions from various market leaders.

After extensive discussions with senior executives and vendors, Forrester defined sales enablement as 'a strategic, ongoing process that equips all client-facing employees with the ability to consistently and systematically have a valuable conversation with the right set of customer stakeholders at each stage of the customer's problem-solving life cycle to optimize the return of investment of the selling system.' This definition focuses on setting up a systematic process to assist sales, so they can have productive conversations with relevant prospects and existing customers. It also highlights the central theme of enabling the sales team with a consistent message and value proposition that connects across the entire sales cycle.

CSO Insights, a research company specializing in sales research, articulated a definition that is widely recognized and accepted in the sales enablement field: 'A strategic, cross-functional discipline designed to increase sales results and productivity by providing integrated content, training and coaching services for salespeople and frontline sales managers along the entire customer's journey, powered by technology.'[5] This definition centres on providing essential technology-based training, organizational socialization (onboarding) and coaching as well as relevant and effective content.

Bray and Sorey say that 'sales enablement is the concept of extending a prospect-focused mindset to all departments within an organization.' In their book *The Sales Enablement Playbook*, they shared a reality to which I can relate: 'The sales enablement position in most cases is like the "Special Projects" role in large organizations, and often it devolves into "Director of Broken Things" – without influence, without budget, without accountability and without charter.' Sales enablement isn't a position; it's an ecosystem that 'crosses all functional and hierarchical boundaries'. Although their book mostly covered training, onboarding, coaching, content and prospecting, which is similar to CSO Insights' definition, they stress that sales enablement is everyone's job.

Hubspot's sales enablement definition focuses on technology and process. 'Sales enablement is the technology, process and content that empowers sales teams to sell efficiently at a higher velocity.'

In summary, there are seven common elements in these definitions:

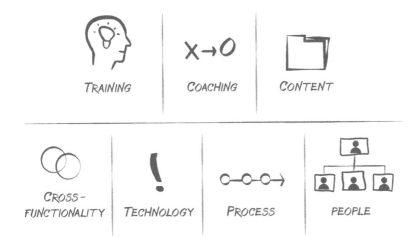

It's all about making sales teams efficient and effective so that they can close sales.

For the purpose of this book, I created my own definition of effective sales enablement: *Deliver a positive customer experience by equipping sales with knowledge, skills, processes and tools through cross-functional collaboration in order to increase sales velocity, sales retention and productivity.*

Most definitions I shared on the previous pages focus on supporting sales and facilitating the purchase process. They are written as one internal team (sales enablement) supporting another internal team (sales). In a digital-first marketing environment, it's crucial to deliver a positive and consistent customer experience both online and offline. That is why it's vital to add the customer to the sales enablement definition. Without customers, there are no sales.

In my definition, knowledge and skills represent content, training and onboarding. Process suggests documented sales processes and methodologies. Tools are software platforms and technologies to implement sales enablement efforts. Increasing sales is important, but sales enablement's role is to also increase sales velocity. Sales velocity is defined as how quickly a product is sold or a deal is closed. By equipping the sales team correctly, marketers align themselves with the goal of increased conversions, thus directly impacting sales results. An effective sales enablement team will, perhaps indirectly, increase sales velocity by removing barriers and friction. Marketing plays a role (as a programme manager) and performs multiple tasks (lead generation campaigns, content creation, etc) as part of the sales enablement process.

0.2

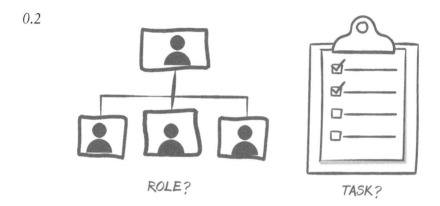

ROLE?   TASK?

Is sales enablement a role or a task?

Forrester convened its first sales enablement executive roundtable in August 2008, facilitated by Scott Santucci. He led the discussion of a 'cross-functional team of VP level executives from sales and marketing roles, representing 16 blue-chip companies like: Accenture, CSC, IBM, CA, Siemens, BMC etc'.

They had an in-depth discussion to assess whether or not sales enablement is a role in itself or a task performed by people in existing roles. They determined that sales enablement is a role, a function within an organization, albeit an emerging and poorly defined one. Forrester subsequently presented the recommendations at five of their conferences and talked to additional executives and vendors to get buy-in.

Although the executives determined that sales enablement is a role, I would argue that sales enablement is both a role and a set of tasks. These vice president (VP)-level executives spoke with a top-down mindset; I'm coming at this with a bottom-up approach. That's why sales enablement is hard to pin down, because of the potential dual roles and different structures. Sales enablement can be performed by an established team, a senior programme manager leading a virtual team, or even just several individual contributors working loosely together. It echoes Ninivaggi's comment that 'sales enablement is still evolving, and the term means different things to different companies'.[6]

Defining sales enablement reminds me of content marketing, a topic with which I am intimately familiar. My first book, *Global Content Marketing*, illustrates how to scale content across regions and countries. Each company treats and defines content marketing differently. Some companies have individual content teams, some embed content marketing elements into different marketing functions. Therefore, the infrastructure of planning and implementing content marketing is different from company to company, and from industry to industry. Whether to organize around roles or specific task implementations heavily depends on an organization's size, sales support structure, the maturity stage of the sales team, and the skills of individuals across the various teams comprising sales and marketing.

Selling technology requires teamwork

Based on my research, the rise of sales enablement is closely correlated with the advancement and complexity of technology. Sales can no longer sell technology products by themselves. This is because technology products usually require explanations, demonstrations and even integrations. Most importantly, selling technology requires TIME for target audiences to understand why they need the technology and how it will solve their problems or enable further success. This makes for a long purchase process. It requires education, persuasion and some coaxing. It's even more complicated to sell technology to enterprises. Employees who source the high-tech products or services generally are not the end-users. The sourcing team are often formed as a research team or task force comprised of various functions. Everyone has a say about which tool or service to purchase. The sales team need to influence a team of buyers, then train a group of users.

The whole purchase cycle gets even more complex when a group of end-users decide to adapt easy-to-use tools based on software as a service (SaaS). That's how Salesforce.com started in many organizations, a small team of people wanted a better CRM solution. The adoption of Slack, Dropbox, Box, etc often was not sanctioned or part of the formal buying process. Technology selling is complicated.

The teamwork approach is further amplified by account-based marketing (ABM). Once sales identify high-value customers or strategic accounts, marketing can define personalized messages, customized content and create integrated campaigns targeted at those accounts. Rather than taking a broad marketing outreach, marketing treats each account as a segment of its own. Each touchpoint along the buyer's journey is personalized to create a better customer experience. Sales and marketing work in tandem on targeted outreach to deliver timely content to the right people in the right context, thus creating a true sense of sales enablement.

Assign an internal programme manager from marketing to support sales

If you look at organizational structures or talk to any relevant managers, you'll find that most marketing managers' roles and responsibilities are external-facing. Even if some roles are internal-facing, such as marketing strategy, operations or analytics, their jobs are primarily to aid outbound marketing. Marketing prioritizes resources and budget toward external communications. By all means, this is the right thing to do.

But, with the primary focus on external communications, marketing may fall short of supporting internal stakeholders, ie the sales team. To be able to better support sales, it's essential for marketing to assign an internal programme manager (or a programme management team if the sales team is big) to foster cooperation and enhance communications between sales and marketing. If you think about it, my role of supporting sales as a marketing manager was really a programme manager disguised as a marketing manager. It's an internal-facing role. The role is not about promoting the value of marketing, it's more about communicating what's going on in marketing and what are key initiatives, campaigns and content that sales need to know, then working together with the sales operations or enablement team. Through regular meetings, the liaison person will know how the sales team is doing and what challenges the team is encountering. This person can use that insight to educate the marketing team about the sales team's needs and challenges and work with different functions of the marketing team to make sure that the sales team is properly supported.

Here are some examples of what sales teams may need from marketing's treasure trove:

1 Potential prospects and deep segmentation.

2 Content for different stages of the buyer's journeys.

3 Marketing research, including social listening and monitoring, on potential accounts or specific prospects.

4 Value propositions by vertical or target accounts.

5 Additional budget requests to run targeted and incremental campaigns for specific outreach.

6 Creative co-marketing and other marketing tactics that can be used in sales negotiations.

7 Training on how to use social media or other marketing tools effectively.

8 Email copy and social media posts for sales outreach.

9 Resources to support joint initiatives.

10 Additional data about leads, prospects and target companies.

The importance of marketing needs to be acknowledged in regular sales meetings. It is not about attending the meeting; marketing should always be a standing agenda item. It doesn't mean that marketing need to provide an update every time; they can always say 'No updates' or 'On track'. But the standing agenda item signals how important it is for sales to understand what marketing are doing and how marketing contribute to sales efforts. Marketing persons who support sales also need to think like a sales rep. A good starting point is to attend onboard and subsequent training classes. There are some prerequisites that I will touch on shortly. Walking a mile in the sales team's shoes will win their respect.

Prerequisites for marketers to support sales

Have a solid go-to-market (GTM) plan

Before supporting sales, marketers need to have their marketing plans in place. They need to understand the marketing objective, metrics, buyer personas, messaging, outreach channels and budget requirements. Nancy Bhagat, segment Chief Marketing Officer and VP of Marketing at TE Connectivity, makes it very clear, 'Marketing is all about selling – whether it's driving awareness and selling the brand, or driving demand for a product or service. It's critical you start with a business strategy and ground your go-to-market activities with your sales goals.' A crisp game plan will help marketers internalize the sales team's needs and incorporate these needs into prospecting and promotion elements of the marketing mix.

Understand the company's business objective and sales strategy

It's easy to support sales by just completing what they ask us to do. They need leads – let's give them leads. They need to be trained – so we will create sales training. We are in the trenches meeting sales' day-to-day needs. But if you want to get ahead of sales and anticipate their needs, you must understand what's important and what will become important (such as new products or new markets) to them and what drives their behaviours. One way to know what's important to them is to have a firm grasp of your company's business objectives, sales strategy, sales targets and prospecting tactics. Business objectives and sales strategy will dictate which products or sales efforts to support. A good sales strategy statement will also answer the question 'Where and how are we going to win?' Thus, it will help marketers and the sales enablement team guide the overall support plan and priorities. In the context of post mortem reviews of won–lost reports, it's beneficial to understand how a deal is lost and adjust strategies and plans accordingly.

Understand the sales process and sales methodology

As marketers supporting the sales team, we need to understand how the sales team works. As well as having knowledge of the sales organization's structure and the different roles of sales team members, it's also essential for those in a marketing function to understand the team's sales processes and methodology.

The sales process is 'the measurable, consistent, and systematic series of steps that map out and track interaction with prospects from their first point of engagement through the closing of an opportunity'.[7] The sales team lays out the steps to engage with their customers based on their understanding of the customer purchase journey (aka buyers' journey). It's very similar to email marketers creating a series of email campaign workflows or campaign managers mapping specific content at different stages of new and existing customer engagement phases.

Sales methodology is 'the learned behaviours, tactics, and strategies used by a sales team to execute and fulfil the sales process in a professional and conversational manner'. A sales methodology includes tools, skillsets and techniques needed to move prospects along the sales funnel.

Some popular sales methodologies

SPIN selling

Situation, Problem, Implication, and Need pay-off. It involves asking questions to understand the buyer's situation, issues and consequences respectively. SPIN focuses the buyer's mind on the pay-off associated with solving their pain points.

Target account selling

is best utilized to manage a sale through a large and complex organization. This approach focuses on breaking down the process into smaller steps, using a strategic plan throughout the life of the sales cycle to be more proactive than reactive.

The challenger sale

breaks sellers up into five buckets: relationship builders, hard workers, lone wolves, reactive problem solvers and challengers. The challengers are the most successful group. They follow a 'teach–tailor–take control' process. They teach their prospects about larger business problems, tailor their communications and take control of the sale by not being afraid to push back on their customers. This approach is best used when selling complex and large-scale B2B solutions.

NEAT selling

Need, Economic impact, Access to authority, Timeline. Determine a prospect's core needs, quantify the economic impact of the related opportunity cost, identify decision makers and qualify the compelling event forcing your prospect to make a decision.

SNAP selling

makes the assumption that everyone is impatient, busy and frazzled. In order to speed up the sales process, you need to keep it simple, being invaluable, always aligning with the needs of the customer, and raise priorities so the customers see your product or service as an urgent requirement. Focus on what is most important to prospects, show your value and make it easy for them to buy.

The Sandler selling system

starts with uncovering the needs of the customer. Then the sales team customize their pitch based on these needs. It emphasizes that both parties (the buyer and the seller) are equally invested in the sales process.

Solution selling

means selling a solution rather than a product. Solution selling has been a foundation for a number of other methodologies as well. It was a reaction to the trend of increasingly complicated offerings.

The value selling framework

is a simple process to manage the conversation with prospects. The methodology develops a mutual understanding regarding how you add value to the buyer and their business. With this conversational framework you compete on value, not price.

Conceptual selling

is founded on the idea that customers don't buy a product or a service but instead buy the concept of a solution that the offering represents. Conceptual selling encourages salespeople to seek to uncover the prospect's concept of their product and understand their decision process rather than open with a sales pitch.

MEDDIC

Metrics, Economic buyer, Decision criteria, Decision process, Identify pain, Champion. It emphasizes a better understanding of your audience and qualifying customers to increase conversions.

SOURCES David Kirk. Sales process or sales methodology: Who cares? https://blog. cloudapps.com/sales-process-sales-methodology.
Emma Brunder. 8 popular sales methodologies summarized. https://blog.hubspot.com/ sales/6-popular-sales-methodologies-summarized

To help explain the differences between sales process and sales methodology, here is an analogy. In sports, there is a pattern to how the game is played. A coach needs to create plans to be ready for the many different potential situations that will be encountered as the game progresses from the start through to the final whistle. Each game has the same rules, but inevitably plays out differently. The game plan and strategy to navigate a particular game are akin to a sales process. A sales methodology is like choosing the specific plays to run at any point in the game based on the situation. Players need the coaches to define and set up the game plan and plays, while coaches need the players to execute the plan and give feedback as the game progresses. This is the type of cross-functional collaboration needed to win!

Understanding your team's processes and methodology is a vital prerequisite to defining how to better support sales. With the understanding on the sales side, you can help define the voice of the customers, align the buyer's journey with the sales processes, and reshape their approach to market. The more you understand how your sales team works, the better you can connect the dots for them. The more you can connect the dots for them, the more you can provide value. The more you can provide value, the more you will earn their respect. The more you earn their respect, the more they will listen and follow your advice. Essentially, you become your sales team's confidant. When I started supporting sales, I made an effort to understand the sales plan, but I was not aware of sales processes and methodology. My support was limited for the first several months, until I had a better grasp of sales processes and methodology.

Remember

Prerequisites for marketers to support sales:

- Have a solid go-to-market plan.
- Comprehend sales process and sales methodology.
- Take sales onboarding and continuous training courses.

Differences between sales operations and sales enablement

Who should present trends to the sales team? Sales enablement, in essence, aids and support sales, but so does sales operations. Sales support structures comes in different shapes and forms, depending on the size of companies, budget, resources, organization structure, maturity of the sales organization and even senior management's preferences. Given that sales enablement is a fairly new term and sales operations have been around for a long time, you'll see different definitions of sales operations and sales enablement. In some organizations, sales enablement is part of sales operations. In others, there are two different groups. I have seen companies that have no official sales enablement group, but the enablement work was done by the product marketing teams in business units. It doesn't matter what the structure is and who does the jobs, they are all *unsung heroes* behind the scenes, taking care of everything.

So, what are the differences between these two groups?

When I talked to Amy Pence, Director of Global Enablement, and Lee Levitt, Manager of Sales Excellence at Oracle, both defined the differences between sales operations and sales enablement in terms of time. Sales operations runs operations and day-to-day activities, compensations and quota, etc. It focuses on the mechanical aspects of sales. Sales enablement is more concerned with equipping salespeople with knowledge, skills and tools; it takes time to build talent and a longer-term view is required. When sales enablement resides in the sales operation team, there is a long-term vs short-term dilemma.

Let's talk about the things that they have in common:

- **Purpose:** Both groups aim to increase the effectiveness and efficiency of the sales team and make it easy for the sales team to do their jobs.

- **Reporting structure:** Usually these two groups report to the head of sales. According to CSO Insights, 53 per cent of the time sales enablement report to sales, and 25 per cent of the time sales enablement and sales operations are in the same group.

- **Accountability:** Both groups share a responsibility for providing sales performance dashboards and analyses in their own areas of expertise.[8]

Even though they may be in the same groups in some organizations, their roles and responsibilities need to be differentiated. Here is one approach to differentiate them.

Sales operations

- sales rep operations: territory planning, deal routing, account assignment, team design
- sales administration: proposal, quoting and contract management, contract governance
- sales incentives and compensation: compensation optimization and administration
- sales pipeline and forecasting: forecast reporting and dashboards
- sales tools and processes: systems and data management such as CRM, configure price quotes (CPQ), sales performance management (SPM), deal desk and discount approvals
- performance analysis related to the above

Sales enablement

- sales onboarding and training, including content, process and training events like sales kick-offs (SKOs)
- content planning, mapping, management and analysis
- sales processes and technologies, including process performance analytics
- sales communication
- customer engagement tools, processes and analysis
- performance analysis related to the above

You can certainly move the roles and responsibilities between the two and add more tasks as you see fit. You can also differentiate sales enablement and sales operations in the buying process. Highspot, a sales enablement platform, suggests that sales enablement is generally concentrated early in the buying process, focusing on training, content and sales processes, whereas sales operations tends to focus later in the buying cycle during the negotiate and close stages. The reality is that it depends on the companies.

With Highspot's approach, the sales enablement professional tends to focus on broader issues such as message and content quality, training and effectiveness of the whole team. Sales operations tends to have many responsibilities that are very detail oriented, such as ensuring that CRM data systems are accurate, forecasting is done properly, and contracts and the closing process are executed correctly. Success in these roles requires vastly different skill sets that can complement each other when properly aligned.

Remember

Although these definitions, roles and responsibilities make sense, companies can still define their own sales enablement organizational structure as they see fit. An effective structure will minimize duplication, enhance collaboration and ensure all responsibilities required to support the sales team are assigned.

Ownership of sales enablement

In addition to the similarities and overlapping responsibilities of sales enablement and sales operations, there are different opinions on where sales enablement should reside. Should sales enablement be part of the sales team, the marketing team or even the business unit/product group? In general, the verdict is that placing sales enablement in the sales team offers the greatest advantage.

Lara Sibley, Senior Director Marketing of Operations and Delivery at CDW, holds the distinct opinion that sales enablement should be part of the marketing team. Her point of view is that prospecting is part of marketing's job anyway. Also, most of the content creation role is fulfilled by marketing. To be more efficient, it makes sense for sales enablement to reside in marketing. For Sibley, who has been doing support on both sides of sales and marketing, her opinion has validity. Curata, whose platform helps you curate, plan, and measure your content marketing efforts, has its sales enablement function in marketing. The primary advantage of placing sales enablement in marketing is to motivate marketing to align with sales at an earlier stage of planning.

The sales enablement function varied from business unit to business unit when I worked at Intel. Some business units owned sales enablement. Other business units had their sales teams manage the sales enablement efforts. Some newly formed groups may not have a sales enablement team per se. However, the responsibilities for product content creation, sales training and subject matter support are handled by different individuals through divisions of labour. Sales people are getting the support they need one way or another.

Remember

The role of sales enablement is constantly morphing, because of reorganizations, product growth and managerial changes. Sales enablement can be in sales, marketing, or product groups as long as a service level agreement is created with the sales team. In addition, there needs to be a sense of 'trust' between the sales and sales enablement team and clear metrics for measuring the effectiveness of sales enablement assets.

Let's get started on how to effectively enable sales.

Notes

1 Brendan Cournoyer. What is sales enablement? 3 definitions that help tell the story. www.brainshark.com/ideas-blog/2013/July/what-is-sales-enablement-3-defintions

2 Elizabeth Gooding. What is 'solutions selling'? 25 March 2011. http://thedigitalnirvana.com/2011/03/what-is-solutions-selling

3 Cory Bray and Hilmon Sorey. *The Sales Enablement Playbook,* CreateSpace Independent Publishing Platform, 2017

4 Scott Santucci. What is sales enablement? And how did Forrester go about defining it? Forrester, 14 August 2010. https://go.forrester.com/blogs/10-08-14-what_is_sales_enablement_and_how_did_forrester_go_about_defining_it

5 Tamara Schenk. CSO Insights sales enablement optimization study. CSO Insights 2016. www.csoinsights.com/wp-content/uploads/sites/5/2016/08/2016-Sales-Enablement-Optimization-Study.pdf

6 Brendan Cournoyer. 5 basic sales enablement questions to ask before 2014. Brainshark, 16 December 2013. www.brainshark.com/ideas-blog/2013/December/basic-sales-enablement-questions-to-ask-before-2014

7 Harris Consulting Group. https://theharrisconsultinggroup.com/sales-process-vs-methodology

8 Jeff Day. Sales enablement and sales operations – one team. Highspot, 8 October 2016. www.highspot.com/articles/sales-operationsw

Sales enablement, Leonardo da Vinci and the Industrial Revolution

Realize that everything connects to everything else.
LEONARDO DA VINCI

I had a sales enablement moment in France when I paid a visit to Leonardo da Vinci's last residence at the Château du Clos Lucé. Perhaps it is strange that when everyone else was simply in awe of Leonardo's imagination, I was thinking about how to market and sell his inventions. But that moment of hypothesizing while standing in his study was the inspiration for this book.

Leonardo used his imagination to design machines that wouldn't be manufacturable for almost five hundred years. I marvelled over his drawings (the flying machine, the automobile) and some of his fearsome military inventions (an assault chariot, a machine gun, a steam canon). As a marketer, I kept wondering: *If he had been able to bring these machines to life and make them work, how would he have marketed and sold his incredible inventions?* How would he have explained the complicated features and benefits in a way that nobles, kings and wealthy merchants could comprehend? What would his show-and-tell demo have looked like? What kind of visual content would he have created to convey his message without the resources to create prototypes? If he had been a savvy business person, would he have built a company, hired a team and dispatched them to different kingdoms and territories to promote his inventions?

Leonardo was so ahead of his time that he was creating objects no one had ever envisioned before, let alone knew how to use in a practical sense. Standing in his study, I contemplated a series of sales and marketing efforts that I'd implement (I imagined myself as his Chief of Staff or VP of Sales or Chief Marketing Officer) if his ideas became viable products that could scale. And the term 'sales enablement' kept popping in to my mind when I was strolling through the Clos Lucé. Wouldn't it be fun to help Leonardo assemble and enable a sales team and sell his creations? *Suddenly, I got excited.*

Then, I asked myself a hypothetical question: 'Would it have been possible to successfully sell Leonardo's creations in his era, the early sixteenth century, if the products were manufactured and a sales team were properly trained?' Well, humans have been selling and buying 'things' and 'stuff' for thousands of years. Selling is not an issue; the issues are the products and buyers.

Then the next two questions came to my mind:

Are my products relevant? During Leonardo's time, most of the goods in transactions were products people needed to eat, wear, live or travel. Although transactional products may also have included art, music and different forms of entertainment or even weapons, products existed to meet their daily needs. Obviously, most of Leonardo's creations were so advanced that they were not directly relevant to people's personal or business essentials.

Are my buyers ready? The so-called 'technologies' used during that time were winches and wedges. Until Leonardo's death in 1512 people still believed that the Earth was the centre of the universe. Galileo didn't publicly announce his belief that the Earth orbits around the Sun until 1632. Acceptance of out-of-the-box thinking and new products was low. And the pool of potential customers that could afford luxuries was small.

As much as I was excited about marketing and selling Leonardo's creations, I quickly analysed the possibilities in my mind and recognized the chances of success were very low. I could convey his vision and put a sales enablement team together to support a sales team that was ready to sell the products, but the products didn't solve the buyers' immediate challenges and the whole ecosystem wasn't ready. I sighed. Leonardo's ideas would remain only ideas in his era.

Then came engines... powered by steam

The tipping point for technology was the Industrial Revolution in the 1700s. For thousands of years, steam from boiling water evaporated in the air, wasting its potential energy. Nobody thought too much of it until Denis Papin. He successfully confined the steam until high pressure was generated, then used a safety valve he invented to release the steam as energy to enable a cylinder and piston to move back and forth. Thomas Savery, a military engineer, saw the challenge of pumping water out of coal mines when the mines became progressively deeper. In the early days, one conventional way of removing water from mines was to use a series of buckets on a pulley system operated by horses. It was slow and expensive. Savery created a steam-powered water pump to remove water from mine shafts in 1698. 'An energetic advertising campaign brought him customers, and he manufactured a number of his engines not only for pumping out mines but also for supplying water to large buildings,' according to the *Encyclopedia Britannica*. It was clear that he was a brilliant inventor as well as a savvy businessman. Savery's water pump had several disadvantages: it could only draw water from shallow depths, and boiler explosions were common due to the primitive design. Savery's version of the steam water pump reminds me of modern start-ups' minimum viable product: the product is good, but is not good enough to scale.

Back in the early 1800s, technology improvements moved at a much slower pace than they do today. Savery certainly didn't have any financial backing. It took another twelve years, until 1712, for the next generation of power pump to come to market. Thomas Newcomen, who is widely credited as the inventor of the steam engine, was an ironmonger (aka blacksmith) by trade. His ironmonger's business included designing, manufacturing and selling machines and tools to the mining industry. His biggest customers were coal-mine owners in Cornwall. Coal-mine owners complained vehemently to Newcomen about the same issue that Savery tried to solve: pumping water out of coal mines. As any salesperson would tell you, the biggest opportunities lie in solving their customers' biggest challenges. Newcomen set out to solve his customers' water pumping challenges by further modifying and improving Savery's design. 'Newcomen's version worked 12 strokes per minutes, raised 10 gallons of water from a depth of 156 feet. The engines were rugged, reliable and worked day and night which is a key factor to make them hugely successful.' Unfortunately, due to Savery's broad patent, Newcomen was forced to partner with Savery to sell his product, despite significant design differences. By the time Newcomen died in 1729, more than one hundred of his steam engines were installed in Britain and across Europe.

Although Savery and Newcomen created a steam engine water pump for coal mining, James Watt took it to the next level by further optimizing their design and inventing a rotary motion for the steam engine. This design could easily apply to other industries such as textiles, paper mills, cotton mills, distilleries, transportation and more. Watt was lucky that he had the financial backing of Matthew Boulton. He had the grand vision of steam engines being employed in almost every industry to enhance productivity. He even applied steam power to coining machinery. He supplied coins for the East India Company and sold machinery to the Royal Mint. By 1800, when Boulton's son took over the business, almost five hundred steam engines were working in Britain and abroad.

More than one hundred of Newcomen's and almost five hundred of Watt's steam engines installed across Europe doesn't sound like a lot in today's terms, but it probably covered all the major mining companies and key industry players in various industries at that time.

Since there was no Silicon Valley venture capital investment infrastructure back then, it took three different people over sixty years (Savery's machine in 1698, Newcomen's design in 1712 and Watt's commercialized design in 1765) to perfect the design and get it adopted by various existing industries. Yet this technology, steam engines, almost single-handedly led to the acceleration of the Industrial Revolution that also guided the invention of new industries such as steam boats, steam trains and massive assembly lines for manufacturing factories for the next two hundred years.

Did we need sales enablement to sell the steam engine?

Steam engines, like Leonardo's creations, were something new. Business owners had never seen the steam engine before, but the key element to success was that the products were relevant and the customers were ready. It was an easy sell for two key reasons:

It was easy to show and tell.   Although it would be hard to explain the technical features to proprietors or business owners and most of them had never seen these machines before, a quick show-and-tell or demonstration easily showcased the products' immediate benefits.

It was easy to quantify savings.   It was also easy to explain and quantify direct cost savings. A mining owner at Griff in Warwickshire needed to employ 500 horses and spent £900 a year to feed and care for the horses in order to drain the water from a deep mine. Business owners could quickly calculate the savings of installing a steam-engine water pump based on the rate of water drainage and cost of maintaining the machines and horses. Even though the up-front cost would be high, the decision was a no-brainer.

Remember

Sales enablement may not be necessary when

- the customer's pain point is acute
- product is relevant to address the pain point
- it's easy to show-and-tell
- it's simple to quantify savings

Despite technology being complicated, involving many components and being challenging to assemble, selling is not difficult if the products are solid and readily solve end users' pains. The steam engine was the right product at the right time. Since the inventor was also the owner, sales manager and maintenance person, the selling process was a lot easier. A separate sales enablement team wasn't needed to sell steam engines.

Selling became complicated after the Industrial Revolution

Alvin Toffler's book *The Third Wave* refers to the Industrial Revolution as the Second Wave. The First Wave was the agrarian revolution during which humans moved to agriculture-based communities from the hunter-gatherer phase. Because of the invention of the steam engine, for the first time in history, humans made the transition from hand-production to machine-production and from manual manufacturing to mass production.[1]

The shift from manual to mass production had a significant impact on almost every aspect of people's daily lives. The factories required massive manpower. Therefore, more and more people left their villages and moved near factories to work, which indirectly formed cities and suburbs. The formation of mega-cities and suburbs led to the creation of 'super' stores. These, in turn, changed how people shopped and purchased products. To improve the cost competitiveness of their products and increase overall margin on items with elastic demand, owners of factories pursued more automated and efficient machines. More machines meant a gigantic pool of upfront capital, which indirectly created the demand for the stock market and banks. The Second Wave created massive, interconnected and complicated systems to manufacture, finance and distribute products to satisfy people's new needs. There are three key elements that impacted the complexity of selling:

Machines powered by machines

The Second Wave pushed technologies to a new level. It spawned gigantic electromechanical machines, moving parts, belts, hoses, bearings, and bolts – all clattering and ratcheting along. According to Toffler, these machines 'could hear, see, and touch with greater accuracy and precision than human beings. [Humans] were able to invent machines that give birth to new machines in infinite progression.' Suddenly, selling newer technologies is powered by existing technologies.

Expanded sales channels

Before the Industrial Revolution, most goods were made by hand and were manufactured on a custom basis. Some goods, such as tea, spice, silk, etc, were distributed by merchants. They opened trade routes around the world, organized by convoys of ships, wagons and camel caravans. The distribution was more linear. After the 1700s products and goods were delivered by sea, railroads, highways and canals. In addition, cities and suburbs created the demand for large-scale outlets such as department stores and supermarkets. Complex networks of wholesalers, commission agents, resellers, channel partners, distributors sprang up. Sales teams needed to engage with different layers of buyers.

The formation of corporations

'As recently as 1800,' says Toffler, 'there were only 335 corporations in the United States, most of them devoted to such quasi-public activities as building canals or running turnpikes.' The rise of mass production changed that completely. Merchants and investors formed corporations to limit their liability and the court treated corporations as 'immortal beings'.Therefore, they could make long-range plans, issue stocks or borrow money and invest capital to build more massive production lines. This introduced a less direct sales process in which a team of buyers acted on behalf of corporations. Industrial marketing was a new requirement, which eventually came to be called business-to-business marketing (B2B).

The ramifications of the Industrial Revolution were profound. No one could have predicted the rippling effects of a steam engine, just as no one would have predicted the impact of social media on language development, modern politics and human interactions. The steam engine impacted how people lived, how purchases were made, and how products were distributed, which led to other changes with further impacts. Those impacts currently include how organizations sell and market their products. In addition to selling directly to potential buyers, a salesperson may need to engage with other channel partners such as wholesalers, resellers, retailers, distributors and trade reps to complete sales. Rather than selling to one decision-maker, sales reps may need to sell to a team of employees in a corporation – a task made more complicated as the products and services became more complex and difficult to comprehend.

Fast-forward to the computer era

According to Oxford Dictionaries, the word *computer* has referred to a person since 1613, to a machine since 1869, and to an electronics device since 1946. Toffler has an interesting analogy to describe how technology begets technology. Toffler stated that humans 'gave technology a womb, by inventing machines designed to give birth to new machines in infinite progression'. Once humans discovered that they could mix and match different components to create new machines and tools – *BAM!* It steadily moved us to the Third Wave, the Information Age.

Ironically, the pace to the Third Wave was also accelerated by World War II and the space race between the United States and the Soviet Union. In order to help break encrypted German military code, the British built the world's first electronic digital programmable computer, Colossus, in 1944. To calculate artillery firing tables for the US Army, John Mauchly and Presper Eckert at the Moore School of Electrical Engineering of the University of Pennsylvania built the Electronic Numerical Integrator and Computer (ENIAC) in 1945. ENIAC could add and subtract five thousand times a second, a thousand times faster than any other machines at that time.

From the 1950s onward, computing made lightning fast improvements compared with the Second Wave. The fascinating history and major milestones are available on the Computer History Museum website, which includes the Timeline of Computer History.[2] You can see all the major milestones and inventions by year. They cover most of the major technology milestones and inventions since 1933.

Sitting in front of my computer, I was browsing through inventions throughout the years on the Timeline of Computer History. If Leonardo da Vinci had been born in the twentieth century, he would fit right in and have the time of his life! He could have taken technology to another level. Just as I was marvelling at Leonardo's creations in Clos Lucé, I was mesmerized by the plethora of innovations over the past eighty years. A question popped into my mind: how could I sell and market new technology-based products? Is sales enablement necessary to sell these innovations?

Sales enablement is ready for prime time

We have come a long way. Just as steam engines created interconnected social systems that changed every aspect of people's lives, big data, artificial intelligence and connected devices will have unforeseeable consequences for years to come. More data was created in 2015 and 2016 than the previous 5,000 years.[3]

I mentioned the three key elements that impacted selling after the Industrial Revolution. They are still valid, but they are morphing along with technologies and customers:

1.2

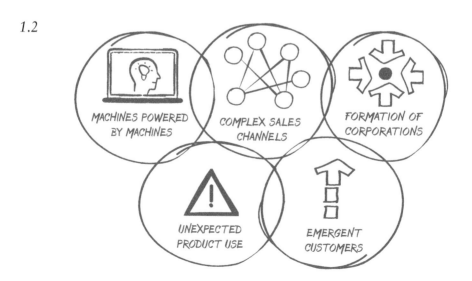

Machines powered by machines: This is quickly transforming into artificial intelligence. Google, Facebook and Uber are training their computers and servers to anticipate our needs with massive amounts of data that we share through their tools and applications.

Complexity of sales channels: Sales channels continue to be fragmented. E-commerce is another sales channel; we can easily incorporate 'buy' buttons into various social channels. There are many sales channels to reach out to your customers and complete sales with or without a sales team.

Formation of corporations: The Internal Revenue Service (IRS), the US tax collection agency, received 32 million business tax return in 2016. The number of companies and enterprises will continue to grow worldwide. And there are a large number of technology-based start-ups created every year. Many of those start-ups are either acquired or merged with other companies. The way you sell to a merged or a new company may need to be different. It makes the sales process even more challenging.

There are two additional key elements to consider:

Unexpected usage of your products: Sometimes you create products for a specific use, but your customers use your products in a different way, which creates new sets of customers. The barcode was originally used for tracking inventory but now we see it being utilized extensively for ticket tracking at events, concerts, movie theatres and even for travel. The YouTube website is not simply a video uploading site; it has become an education destination used to acquire new skills and obtain new knowledge.

Emergent customers from new and existing verticals: Your products may create new verticals and new accounts that you don't initially know how to reach. A company that manufactures touch screens intended for smartphones may recognize that the same technology can also scale to other existing verticals such as TV, medical devices, computer and automobile segments. Touch screen technology can also be meshed with augmented reality (new vertical segment) as a dual-purpose TV monitor and mirror at retail stores so that shoppers can visualize how clothes will look on them without trying them on. With new technologies, opportunities are endless.

Remember

Key elements that impact selling after the Industrial Revolution

- machines powered by machines
- fragmented sales channels
- growth of new companies
- unexpected usage of products
- creation of new verticals

I also mentioned earlier that the products need to be relevant and the customers need to be ready. However, these two rules are changing in the twenty-first century. Many new products were created when they may have seemed irrelevant and the customers were not ready. Think of the PC. When the personal computer was created, it didn't immediately take off. From Xerox Alto in 1973, MITS Altair 8800 in 1975, Altari 400 in 1978 to IBM PC in 1982, different versions of PCs didn't seem to be relevant and customers were not ready. It took about 17 years for the PC (from 1973 to 1989) to hit 50 million units in the US. The pace was much faster for the iPhone. It took less than four years to hit 50 million units worldwide.

Eric Schmidt, Executive Chairman of Alphabet and former CEO of Google, said it nicely: 'I spend most of my time assuming the world is not ready for the technology revolution that will be happening to them soon.'[4] Even though the world is not ready, you can still create demand for your products and educate your customers to make them ready, but the lack of demand or customer readiness should not stop you from experimenting and piloting new products and technologies. If you are selling technology products or exploring new product categories, sales enablement is especially critical to the success of the sales team. It takes a village to sell technology.

With so many different moving pieces, technology selling is harder than ever before. Your sales personnel are like soldiers on the front line. As they move forward, the supplies of food, fuel, tools and logistics need to keep up with the solders in order to enable them to achieve their final objectives. Sales enablement are the supply team that stands behind the sales team to make sure they have everything they need. Sales enablement, along with sales processes and sales methodology, is finally ready for prime time.

What you can do

1 Describe your company's sales processes and sales methodology.

2 Define sales enablement in the context of your role and your company.

3 Based on your understanding of sales processes and methodology, and your own definition of sales enablement, identify three areas in which you can further help your sales team.

Notes

1 Alvin Toffler. *The Third Wave*, Bantam Books, New York, 1980

2 Timeline of Computer History. www.computerhistory.org/timeline/year

3 Richard Harris. More data will be created in 2017 than the previous 5,000 years of humanity. 23 December 2016. https://appdevelopermagazine.com/4773/2016/12/23/more-data-will-be-created-in-2017-than-the-previous-5,000-years-of-humanity-/ [Blog] App Developer Magazine

4 M G Siegler. Eric Schmidt: every 2 days we create as much information as we did up to 2003. TechCrunch, 20 November 2010. https://techcrunch.com/2010/08/04/schmidt-data

Twelve sales trends that matter 02

*The modern sales professional is actually not a seller
but is someone who helps people buy.*
JILL ROWLEY, CHIEF GROWTH OFFICER, MARKETO

Understanding trends is a vital part of business planning. In most of the strategy decks I've seen, a section about 'megatrends' research or 'SWOT' analysis (strength, weakness, opportunity and threat) is indispensable. These analyses are included because an examination of external elements, such as opportunities and threats, needs to be factored into shaping critical business decisions.

My son, Aaron, has always been a practical child. When he was evaluating his college major, he went online to research the technology trends and potential job opportunities in different fields. He noticed that almost everything is built on software or some sort of code. He believes that the world will continue to be built on software and code, and therefore a profession such as a software engineer or programmer will always be in high demand. In addition, no matter what one does, it will be beneficial to know how to program or code. So, he ticked the 'computer science' box instead of 'accounting' on his college application, based on his trend analysis. Then, he modified his behaviour and started focusing on programming and coding. He also identified challenges that he needed to overcome in order to be a successful software programmer, such as the classes he needs to take, the programming languages he needs to learn, and the credentials that he will need to build over time. He tackled these goals one by one. No fuss.

I told him that he was pretty shrewd to have reached the same conclusion as Marc Andreessen: 'Software is eating the world.'[1] As my son said matter-of-factly: 'You need to understand where the world is going, Mom.' True! I especially like his simple approach, which can be summarized in five points:

.1

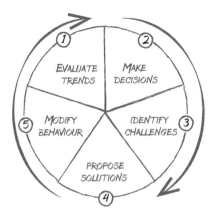

In the business world, we follow a similar approach. High-level decisions are made by senior executives based on future megatrends, middle management and individual contributors identify challenges and find solutions to them. Often, it will require reorganization, a change to workflows, or modification of employees' behaviour, and sometimes all of the above.

Of course, you can also identify a trend but make the decision to disregard it. This often happens when a trend is not really a trend, but a short-lived buzz or fad. For example: augmented reality is a trend, while Pokémon Go was a fad. Augmented reality is a trend that's not going away. Ways to incorporate augmented reality into digital interactive learning must be part of long-term training discussions, but a conversation about creating a Pokémon Go-like learning environment is not necessarily a trend discussion. You need to comprehend where the trend is going in order to decide whether or not it applies to your business. None of this is possible, though, without understanding the trends themselves.

Remember

Know the difference between a trend and a fad. Make decisions by understanding where the world is going, then you can decide if you want to go with the flow or go against it.

The sales world is changing rapidly

The steps that go into closing a sale have not changed much. You must establish relationships with prospects, earn their trust, persuade them to take action, maintain the relationship and retain the customer. What has changed is the world surrounding sales professionals. Elements such as market dynamics, sophisticated and educated buyers, customer expectations and disruptive technologies are now uncontrollable factors that are 'fomenting a perfect storm of trends that are changing the context of how sellers and buyers interact with one another, how they share information, and how they make decisions'.[2]

From trends to solutions: start with *Why?*

Here is the challenging part: salespeople hate change. They are set in their ways and want to repeat whatever worked in the past. I loved my sales team, but modifying their behaviour could sometimes feel like moving mountains. I have been successful in getting my sales team to adopt some of my initiatives, but I have also worked on process changes that failed miserably. In their defence, the sales team had a lot going on. Changing behaviours is not their priority; therefore, modifying their behaviours and implementing new processes requires patience, time, effort and continuous follow-up. There is no way around it.

I discovered that *explaining why* is usually a good starting point to initiate a conversation about changes. Simon Sinek, author of *Start with Why*, has a similar opinion.[3] He stated that the *why* is the purpose, cause or belief that inspires you and your team to do what you do. And the best way to explain the *why* is to start sharing the trends. It's not about any trends, it's about trends that will impact the salespeople. Sales teams care most about their commissions. How will they drive their sales up to increase their income? By understanding the trends that are changing their customers' needs, wants and behaviours, they will know what they should change to keep up with their customers.

Key trends that shape the sales profession

While researching trends that are likely to impact the future of sales professionals and support efforts, I found a very comprehensive list in *Success in Selling: Developing a world-class sales ecosystem*. Reza Sisakhti, Managing Director of Productivity Dynamics, and his team interviewed 59 thought leaders and 259 sales professionals from different verticals, industries and regions around the world. His research and findings identified twelve trends that shape today's sales profession. If our role as marketers is to support the sales team, it's imperative to understand the trends so that we can make the necessary adjustments to help them change.

It's critical to understand all of these trends, which Sisakhti organized into four categories:

2.2

MARKET DYNAMICS & CHANGING CUSTOMER DEMAND	ADVANCES IN TECHNOLOGY	WORKFORCE RECONFIGURATION	SALES TALENT DEVELOPMENT
1 Rise of empowered buyers	**6** On-demand availability	**9** Multigenerational sales teams and customer teams	**11** Use of analytics to gain leaner insights
2 Sales force verticalization	**7** Omnipresent social media	**10** Globalization of teams and customer base	**12** Emergence of integrated learning environments as a necessity
3 Shift from 'FAB' to 'solution' to 'insight' selling	**8** Analytics-based prospecting		
4 Blurred lines between sales and marketing			
5 Adoption of hybrid sales communications			

Rise of empowered buyers

Today's tech-savvy customers continue to educate themselves about products and services by accessing a wide array of information on the Internet. Keith Eades and Timothy Sullivan referred to this as 'Buyer 2.0' in their book *The Collaborative Sale*.[4] According to them, there are fundamental changes in buyer behaviour:

1 Buyers prefer performing their own research by comparing products/services, reading online reviews and getting peer reviews from social media channels.

2 Buyers are delaying the involvement of sellers in their buying process.

3 More people are involved in purchase decisions: buying by committee is more common than ever before.

4 Buyers have developed a higher aversion to risk, resulting in more decisions to do nothing or to simply maintain the status quo.

5 Buyers are asserting more formalized control over their purchasing processes and are demanding greater seller transparency.

Millennial buyers will set new standards for conducting extensive research on their own and further delaying the engagement of sellers in the buying process. They are also comparison and value shoppers. They do their homework; the challenge is how to provide additional value to well-educated buyers.

Challenges

Buyers often do a great deal of research on their own and make purchase decisions without involving a sales team, even in B2B business transactions.

Potential solutions

- Be present, online and offline, as a credible source of information when buyers do their homework. They continuously seek information about solutions and are exposed to trends by their peers through social media. This put a lot of pressure on both marketing and sales to work together. For targeted strategic accounts, account-based marketing can address this issue. For smaller accounts, content marketing coupled with search optimization is an option.

- The sales team need to move upstream to proactively research and target prospects and initiate interest-building engagement for their business needs and opportunities.

- Understand the roles and responsibilities of committee-driven teams, especially in B2B enterprise selling. Be prepared to share more information, such as the future product roadmap, post-sales support structure, the origin of raw materials, even the product cost structure.

Sales force verticalization

Armed with knowledge, empowered buyers increasingly have a low tolerance for a generalist type of salesperson who focuses on horizontal sales. They expect the salesperson to be an expert or a specialist who understands the industry dynamics, major challenges, business opportunities and competitive landscape. It's about providing 'business process improvement as opposed to the recitation of standard generic product features and functions to customers'.[5]

Challenges

Buyers expect sellers to have vertical-specific expertise. Solutions and recommendations need to be customized or vertical-specific.

Potential solutions

- Sales enablement needs to be narrowly focused and vertically specific with content/messaging for each specific vertical. Organizations need to create a matrix of messaging, content, value propositions by vertical segment and make sure each vertical has the required items.

Shift from 'FAB' to 'solution' to 'insight' selling

Since empowered buyers don't care for a generalist type of seller or a generalized sales process, they are certainly less interested in straight features, advantages and benefits (FAB) selling. Solution selling came to play in the late 1970s and early 1980s. Sales teams focus on the customer's problems and address the issue with appropriate offerings of product and services (AKA solutions). If you think back to Chapter 1, this is why Thomas Savery started to build the steam engine. It's about solving miners' problem of pumping water out of coal mines. Little did he know that his invention directly changed how society functioned for the next two hundred years. Insight selling takes this one step further: it's not about trying to meet customers' existing needs, it's about redefining them and revealing customers' needs that they don't even know they have.[6] Be one step ahead of your customers.

Challenges

Buyers expect sellers to provide customized and personalized FAB. Buyers expect sellers to be more than sales persons. They expect sellers to be thought leaders, consultants, coaches and much more.

Potential solutions

- Customized value propositions are necessary. It's also essential for sales to conduct research and analysis to gain in-depth understanding of customers' needs and uncover new challenges and opportunities. I will discuss this further in Chapter 4, which considers brand and messaging.

- Challenge customers' status quo, ask thought-provoking questions and explore alternatives and best courses of action with the customers' interests foremost. All of the various sales methodologies I summarized in the Introduction chapter, SPIN selling, challenger sale, Sandler selling, solution-based and more, emphasize asking questions and understanding customer needs.

Blurred lines between sales and marketing

In the past, sales and marketing had clearly defined roles and responsibilities. With the rise of digital and social media, which lowered the barrier of entry for many to 'self-market' or use these tools as part of their sales process, these two functions are becoming blurred. Email was used mostly by marketing; now sales can run their own mini-email campaigns from sales enablement or CRM tools. Lead generation was mostly the job of marketing or business development managers (BDM) – now any sales person can easily prospect and qualify leads simply by using LinkedIn and other tools. Prospect outreach is not just marketing's job anymore.

Challenges

Since both sales and marketing are doing outreach, there are risks of inconsistent customer experience, confusion, duplication, inefficiency and intrusiveness.

Potential solutions

- Sales and marketing need to align on their digital footprint to deliver a seamless experience and avoid duplication and inefficiency. To do so, it's important to have tools and processes in place to guide and align sales and marketing efforts. CRM and a synchronized marketing automation system are the minimal requirements. You need to build your marketing and sales technology stack based on sales processes and the buyer's journey.
- Sales and marketing need to collaborate to align their game plans on how to engage potential prospects at the right stage with the right blend of content and value propositions. Again, this is critical for an account-based approach.

Adoption of hybrid sales communications

Empowered buyers, especially Millennials, are accustomed to texting, using mobile apps or communicating using social media channels, Facetime meetings, video conferencing and screen sharing. If they have questions, they would like to reach out to their sales contacts with their preferred media at their preferred time. In addition, more and more organizations restrict corporate travel and embrace cost-effective and virtual sales communications. Sales professionals need to understand that face-to-face meetings are not the only way to reach customers. Customer engagements move back and forth between online and offline throughout the purchase journey.

Challenges

Salespeople may not be aware of the latest types of communications tools from social media channels – Google hangouts, Slack, Zoom, video conferencing tools and many others. Some buyers are only reachable through specific social media channels.

Potential solutions

- Salespeople need to enhance online communication fluency using both conventional and virtual channels including, but not limited to, WebEx, LinkedIn, Facebook, Skype, Zoom Meetings, WhatsApp, WeChat and whatever virtual communications their prospects have become accustomed to using.

On-demand availability

Virtual communications can certainly reduce costs and improve productivity and communications. Some buyers may expect sellers to be available at all times and to respond immediately. Others may appreciate digital communications and consider an unanticipated phone call to be interruptive.

Challenges

Sellers who manage many accounts may lack understanding of customers' communications preferences. Digital communications are convoluted. It's challenging to create a communication process that is easy for the sales team to follow. This may be difficult to manage from account to account when adopting buyers' preferred communications channels.

Potential solutions

- Set up expectations for customer response time and methods of communications. Create dos and don'ts of 24/7 communications to avoid burnout and communications fatigue. Make it part of onboarding and continuous training.

- Sales tools such as sales portals or sales collaboration platforms need to be easily accessible through smart phones, tablets and even digital watches. Mobile access to sales information should not be an after-thought.

- Due to frequent on-demand communications, you may need to send files or confidential information using third party tools. It's important to follow proper steps to safeguard customers' confidential information (eg prevent the sending of confidential information via texting or third-party mobile apps) and avoid improper use or overuse of mobile technology (eg avoid being intrusive to customers). A company guideline is essential.

Omnipresent social media

Increasingly, empowered buyers share their issues, concerns and opinions on social media, online forums and communities for all to see. Social media allows sales to 'listen' to and 'engage' with prospects. Sales can easily monitor and make appropriate comments and contributions to foster relationships.

Challenges

Even though social media may come easily to some sales professionals, it takes time and effort to do social media outreach right. In addition, salespeople may not have time to use social media in a disciplined manner and can be overwhelmed by the many social media tools out there. Social media outreach is also embedded into CRM and other tools. It can be confusing and difficult to decide on the best tools for engaging with prospects.

Potential solutions

- It's increasingly vital for sales to be available via social media channels. The challenge is that social media tools are updated and refreshed frequently; Facebook often adds new features, LinkedIn incorporates new lead-generation tools. Social media tools don't stay static. Sales teams need continuous education on new features from sales enablement, sales training or marketing teams. In addition, it's important to make marketing content easy to access for salespeople. Marketing can supply content and social media tool-kits or cheat sheets for social media posts.

Analytics-based prospecting

Powerful pipeline and CRM applications, along with big-data mining and artificial intelligence, are changing the way sellers target and engage with customers. The integration and correlation of customer data from sales, CRM, customer service, websites and social media can help to develop a more sophisticated understanding of your customers. This, in turn, improves the quality of pipelines and prospects, identifies potential opportunities for cross-selling, and optimizes pricing and forecasting.

Challenges

Plenty of data is scattered around a company; the challenge is to sift through it to find insights for sales to act upon. In addition, it takes time to conduct in-depth analysis in order to find actionable insights. The questions are: Who should conduct the analysis? Should we use tools with built-in intelligence or should we hire data analysts? Either way, back-end infrastructure needs to be integrated.

In addition, the customer information that is collected has to be used wisely and it requires education to ensure the sales team are aware of proper ways to handle it.

Potential solutions

- To find actionable insights in corporate data, sales organizations need to have tools in place and possibly hire data analysts to conduct analysis as part of the sales or marketing team.
- A workflow and methodology for data-based prospecting needs to be established. Data correlation and analysis need to be optimized and reviewed on a regular basis. Expected key performance indicators (KPIs) and a service level agreement (SLA) need to be established to ensure salespeople respond to requests and activity triggers in a timely manner.

- Marketing can also supply data modelling such as 'propensity to buy' based on its own customer purchasing behaviour and insights.

- It's important to evaluate the sales and marketing technology stack and add tools to align sales processes and the purchase journey. Add lead services using Data.com, RainKing, DiscoverOrg or other tools as necessary.

Multigenerational sales teams and customer teams

Both the sales team and their prospects comprise Baby Boomers (born 1946 to 1964), Generation X (1965 to 1980) and Millennials (1981 to 2000). In terms of size, Millennials are now the largest generation across the globe. While the youngest Baby Boomers are in their early 50s in 2018, these three generations are likely to coexist in professional settings for the next decade. Generational traits such as work habits, behaviour attributes, tech savviness, content consumption channels and decision-making process are distinctively different. While sellers are working closely with customers, they are likely to encounter a committee or a team composed of all three generations.

Challenges

Internally, creating value propositions and content that will resonate with three generations is the first challenge. Externally, having buyer personas that account for difference in all three generations is another. Therefore, it's vital to understand working dynamics.

Potential solutions

- In addition to gaining vertical-specific expertise, salespeople also need to be aware of the behavioural differences and key characteristics of these generations. Build and incorporate essential tactics for working effectively with generational differences. When you build a sales playbook, it's important to take into account talking points and content for multi-generational preferences. For example: Baby Boomers and Generation X may prefer proper PowerPoint presentation during face-to-face meetings, while Millennials are likely to use whiteboarding (shared files on an onscreen shared notebook or whiteboard) during meetings.

- Sales organizations will also encounter the challenges of assimilating and training Millennials and organizing a cohesive sales organization encompassing three generations.

Food for thought: sales professionals may be able to draw on their internal experience of integrating the younger generation into the team. You can also empower the younger team members to influence decisions regarding engaging with their generation. Companies with a younger staff shouldn't ignore the value of having some Baby Boomers on staff to help with engaging that generation. Conversely, younger companies primarily staffed by Millennials shouldn't underestimate the value of having more experienced Baby Boomers on the team, both to help understand tried and tested tactics and to relate to purchasing teams in more established companies.

Globalization of teams and customer base

Current political tides seem to be focused on localism and separatism, from Quebec seeking independence from Canada in 1995 to Britain's decision to leave the European Union in 2016 to the Catalan independence movement in Spain in 2017. Although some governments continue to create trade tariffs and other regulations to prevent the free flow of goods and services, commerce and trade continues to flourish without boundaries by advances in the Internet, virtual communications and e-commerce. The world economy's interconnectedness is accelerating. Globalization never stops. To standardize processes and tools, multinational companies (MNCs) create global sales teams and global purchasing committees in which decisions are made in a distributed but unified manner.

Challenges

Although most established sales organizations have processes and methodologies in place, the sales team needs to have a game plan and support structure to engage with MNC accounts. Another consideration is having sales support on the ground in priority countries.

Potential solutions

- When dealing with a global purchase committee that includes members from multiple countries, the sales team needs to find a balance of global vs local or headquarters vs geographies (geos).

- As if verticalization and multi-generational customers are not complicated enough, sales teams need to take into account cultural, social and language differences so that messaging is conveyed correctly and professionally. This adds another layer of complexity if you pursue personalized or account-based selling. Take into account content translation and localization to increase the probability of conversions.

Use analytics to gain learner insights

Timely training and onboarding are key to your sales team's success. Equip them with knowledge, skills, processes and tools to get them ready to win over customers. With tablets, smartphones and wearables (using smartwatches to receive short, concise product tips), training managers can track key performance indicators related to sales and training materials. With big data and advanced analytics, it's possible to extract valuable information from the sales team by studying their learning patterns and behaviours.

Challenges

The key is to establish both quantitative and qualitative digital training dashboards. A feedback loop needs to be in place to optimize and improve the quality of training content. Another consideration is that training needs to be scaled to the devices that the sales team uses. Design and user interface are critical factors to consider.

Potential solutions

- With digital, everything is trackable. Establish a process to monitor and track training downloads and usage. Create a process to gather feedback from the sales team through interviews and online surveys.

- Use advanced platforms and tools to integrate intuitive and user-friendly designs into training. It's easier said than done, but it's important to frequently review different training platforms. Design and user-friendly interface are critical for continuous and online learning.

Emergence of integrated learning environments as a necessity

Learning is not confined to classrooms or simply downloading materials to 'read' or 'study'. It's important to create a 'learning environment' so that sales can learn both formally and informally. The formal learning can be via classroom setting, webinars or reading materials, which a lot of companies are doing already. Informal learning can involve listening to a podcast, contributing to a blog post, reading a quick SMS text on a smart watch or viewing a short video while in a cab. All this on-the-go learning can be incentivized through a gamification approach by encouraging salespeople to earn points, badges or awards in a game-like environment. The secret is to construct the knowledge in a way that is easy for sales to absorb.

Challenges

Learning is anywhere and anytime. Space and time don't matter any more. Training managers need to rethink how to structure and deliver training. Sales managers need to relearn how to attain knowledge digitally.

Potential solutions

- Identify learning channels for formal and informal training. Map editorial topics and content formats to these channels.
- Incorporate gamification to support role plays in a virtual world. Use technologies to enable crowd learning – the collaborative use of peer knowledge in real time. Optimize mobile learning and video usage.

The benefits of understanding trends

Trends help you to identify future opportunities. They also help you to gauge customer behaviour, market landscape, technology advancement, workforce configuration and more. You can also use trends to identify areas that need to be addressed. On the flip side: if you have certain initiatives that you would like to push, you can pick and choose the relevant trends to validate your recommendations. It's also important to map trends to actionable business outcomes for customers.

So, understanding trends can help you to:

- explain why
- identify challenges and propose initiatives to support the sales teams
- substantiate your initiatives and stay the course

2.3

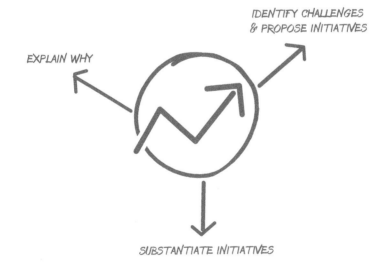

EXPLAIN WHY

IDENTIFY CHALLENGES
& PROPOSE INITIATIVES

SUBSTANTIATE INITIATIVES

Next steps after identifying initiatives

If we follow my son's approach, the next step after identifying challenges and solutions is to modify behaviours. That makes sense for him. But in the corporate world it's not as simple as that.

Very likely, you'll need to present your solutions to internal stakeholders to get buy-in. Here is a modified approach for companies:

- Identify challenges.

- Prioritize solutions.

- Obtain buy-in.

- Implement recommendations.

- Modify behaviours.

- Measure success.

- Monitor performance.

- Comprehend trends.

- Rinse and repeat – it's a continuous cycle.

2.4

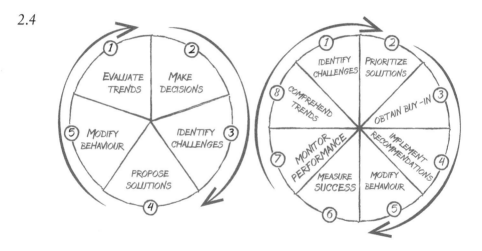

Also, resources and budget play a critical role; you may need to prioritize your recommendations and focus on one initiative at a time, or have several teams working in parallel. It's a collaborative effort. Start to understand the trends, identify the gaps, propose solutions, implement tools and processes and work with the sales team to get through the learning curve and help them to be productive. It's important to break initiatives down into implementable phases. Too often these turn into mega projects that take too long, cost too much, and never get out of the door. There needs to be a vision and roadmap but with discreet deliverables or minimal viable products that deliver visible value along the way.

Salespeople need to be more than salespeople

Have you noticed the job titles of many career professionals don't really describe their jobs anymore? I love talking to Lisa and Mike, sales specialists in the Apple and Microsoft stores in the Washington Square Mall near my house. Again, they are not just salespeople, they are IT tech support, customer services and product experts. They are trained to 'sell' products to us. According to the Apple website as of November 2017, a sales specialist's job is to 'transform Apple Store visitors [into] loyal Apple customers'. At end of the day, it's still about business: increase sales velocity, close sales and drive cross-sell and up-sell. Problem solving is just a means to close deals. Salespeople are problem solvers in disguise. Most of the time, they are sincere, genuine and willing to help in all possible ways. I know they also want me to buy the latest phone, watches and devices, but they make an effort to solve my problems first. You need to make a difference to your customers when you engage with them. It's no longer about selling, it's about educating and conversing.

Jonathan is a shoe salesman in Nordstrom, a department store that is well known for its impeccable customer service and generous return policy. To me, he is not just a shoe salesman, he is my personal shoe stylist. He knows my style and preferences well. When I arrive, he'll bring me two dozen pairs of shoes that he knows I'll like. Buying shoes from him is such a pleasant and easy experience. Occasionally, he'll also nudge me to wear something out of my comfort zone, like a pair of bright red high-heels. Yes, I bought my first pair of red high-heels because of his recommendation.

The commonality of Jonathan in Nordstrom, and Lisa and Mike in the Apple and Microsoft stores is that they all wear multiple hats. Selling becomes secondary; they are first and foremost problem solvers. I see a similar shift in B2B sales. Customers expect sales to be a solution solver, thought leader, subject matter expert, and partner first while the role of salesman only comes into play later.

I agree with Jill Rowley's quote at the beginning of this chapter. It's not about selling, it's about *helping* people buy. It's about uncovering their needs and facilitating their thinking and decision-making process. Nothing more and nothing less. Millennials believe that the world is increasingly unstable, but they also have reason to believe that, by working together, there is hope of improving performance of both business and society as a whole. For us, it's time to know where the world is going and to do something about it.

What you can do

1 List the top five trends that will shape the future of your sales team.

2 Identify three proposed solutions based on the top five trends.

3 Compare the top three proposed solutions from Chapter 2 with the top three thoughts from Chapter 1. Are they similar or different? Why?

Notes

1 Marc Andreesen. Why software is eating the world. *Wall Street Journal*, 8 November 2011. www.wsj.com/articles/SB10001424053111 90348090457651225091562946O

2 Reza Sisakhti. *Success in Selling: Developing a world-class sales ecosystem*, ATD, Virginia, USA, 2017

3 Simon Sinek. *Start With Why: How great leaders inspire everyone to take action*, Penguin, New York, 2011

4 M Keith Eades and Timothy T Sullivan. *The Collaborative Sale: Solution selling in a buyer-driven world*, Wiley, Hoboken, US, 2017

5 Steve W Martin. Top 10 Sales Trends for 2013. *Harvard Business Review*, 12 October 2012. https://hbr.org/2012/12/top-10-sales-trends-for-2013

6 Brent Adamson, Matthew Dixon and Nicholas Toman. The end of solution sales. *Harvard Business Review*, July–August 2012. https://hbr.org/2012/07/the-end-of-solution-sales

The dilemma for marketing as a sales enablement function

03

What's a tip for working with sales? Do what you do best: build brand love, loyalty, and conversions.
ALANA ZAMORA, HEAD OF CONTENT MARKETING, MEDALLIA

Depending on who you talk to and what their first-hand experiences are, the dynamics of the sales and marketing relationship range from being as tumultuous as fire and ice, to being as perfectly matched as fish and water. It's that love–hate relationship. Sales teams need marketing's help and marketing teams need sales results to validate their existence. When the boundary between the two groups starts to disappear, sales becomes one of the marketing channels. Marketing becomes a hidden sales force.

I didn't know it at that time, but this book reunited two friends who had not talked for five years. Alana Zamora and I worked together when we were at Intel. She joined Intel from Oracle and was the Global Media Manager leading Intel's global media planning and campaigns. I was responsible for crafting a global go-to-market plan for Intel's enterprise segment (B2B marketing). Since media buying is a critical part of the go-to-market plan, she and I worked together on annual global media briefs several times. She went on and joined Google, while I continued at Intel. We stayed in touch initially, then we both got busy and didn't talk for five years until I needed a big favour.

While planning a family trip to northern California it occurred to me that, since my two boys are studying computer science, it would be great for them to visit a couple of technology companies while we were there. We had a chance to do our sightseeing in San Francisco, and I thought we might as well also sightsee some great companies to get a sense of the workplace, the corporate culture, even their hiring philosophy.

Google naturally came to my mind. Not having talked to Alana for five years, the first 'How are you' email was actually a Can-you-give-my-sons-a-Google-tour request. As gracious as she has always been, she responded to my email almost immediately and was happy to show my boys the Google campus. When we met, she told me about her amazing experiences over the past five years. Her job took her to the United Kingdom and Ireland, and when she came back to the US she took on a sales enablement role at Google's YouTube division. *What?* I told her that I had been thinking about making the topic of sales enablement as my second book, but that it would be written from a marketer's perspective. Who knew that asking her to give my sons a Google tour would result in finding a great subject matter expert that could give input into my book? Our conversation that day, and subsequent exchanges, sparked our collaboration for this chapter.

Marketing is woven into the solutions of future trends

In order to understand the role of marketing in sales enablement, we reviewed Reza Sisakhti's sales trends, summarized in Chapter 2, and tried to define marketing's possible role in the proposed solutions. We wanted to see if marketing could assist in providing the proposed solutions for each trend.

It can.

As you can see in the table on page 54, marketing's role is part of every solution, no matter how different trends shape the future of sales. In a way, marketing's role is indispensable to sales. Sales teams need to stay even closer in the future, yet the constant tension and conflict of goals and priorities draw them apart. Their dynamics ebb and flow. It's never the same.

Constant friction between sales and marketing

Alana and I loved our sales teams but found it almost impossible to please them. We agree wholeheartedly that sales is a high-pressure job. Salespeople are under a lot of stress to meet quotas, convert quickly, retain customers, grow the lifetime value of each customer and, most importantly, make sure they get paid. They are constantly analysing their business to identify the biggest opportunities and risks – carefully managing pipelines and moving opportunities around like chess pieces to secure high-profit contracts at the right time of the quarter and year. It's a tough job. As marketers, we feel their pain.

We also agree that the sales team can't manage everything from pipeline to the final sales stages alone. To start with, marketing helps sales by promoting the business's or product's core value propositions through mass media channels to build product and service awareness. The challenge is that sales and management won't see the benefits of this mass marketing instantly, yet they need to meet monthly and quarterly quotas. Some marketing efforts are intended as long-term plays, while sales are constrained to meet short-term goals. The dilemma of meeting long-term vs short-term goals is a constant source of friction.

Although the long-term vs short-term dilemma can be addressed by account-based marketing (ABM), in which marketing works closely with sales to leverage customized and personalized marketing outreach for targeted accounts, it's hard to scale ABM effectively to many accounts and build mass brand awareness solely with ABM.

In addition, no matter what marketers do, it just doesn't seem to be good enough. When I talked to other marketers who work in different industries and verticals, we all share the same sentiment. I am sure when salespeople get together and talk about marketing, they commiserate too.

▶ *continues on page 58*

Marketing: trends and solutions

Sales trend	Proposed solution	Marketing functions
Rise of empowered buyers: rather than depending on sellers to provide information, buyers educate themselves on how various solutions solve their problems	• Be present, online and offline, as a credible source of information when buyers do their homework. They continuously seek information about solutions and are exposed to trends of their peers through social media. • The sales team need to move upstream proactively to research and target prospects and initiate interest-building engagement for their business needs and opportunities. • Understand the roles and responsibilities of committee-driven members. Be prepared to share more information, such as the future product roadmap, post-sales support structure, the origin of raw materials, even the product cost structure.	• Marketing can provide relevant and credible content online and offline. • Marketing can find opportunities to help sales move upstream in the purchase funnel. • Marketing can help sales with account-based selling and provide information for consensus-driven buying.
Sales force verticalization: buyers' needs are increasingly becoming more vertical-centric.	• Build vertical-specific acumen within the sales team. Tailor product-specific value propositions and build relevant content for target verticals.	• Marketing can define vertical-specific personas and create vertical-specific value propositions and content.
Shift from 'FAB' to 'solution' to 'insight' selling: buyers expects sellers to address the known and uncover unknown problems.	• Customized value propositions are necessary. It's also essential for sales to conduct research and analysis to gain an in-depth understanding of customers' needs and uncover new challenges and opportunities. • Challenge customers' status quo, ask thought-provoking questions and explore alternatives and best courses of action with the customers' interests foremost.	• Marketing can work with sales to uncover customers' needs. • Marketing can help sales on positioning. • Marketing can create case studies to support solution and insight selling.

Blurred lines between sales and marketing: sales and marketing use the same tools to reach out to customers.

- Sales and marketing need to align on their digital footprint to deliver a seamless experience and avoid duplication and inefficiency.
- Sales and marketing need to collaborate to align their game plans on how to engage potential prospects at the right stage with the right blend of content and value propositions.
  - Marketing need to share their plans and strategy and align with the sales team.
  - Marketing can collaborate with the sales team to enhance sales velocity using marketing programmes.
  - Sales and marketing can share tools (CRM) to make coordination and collaboration easier.

Adoption of hybrid sales communications: leverage online and offline or buyers' preferred communications channels to engage with customers and prospects.

- Salespeople need to enhance online communication fluency using both conventional and virtual channels, including, but not limited to, blogs, LinkedIn, Facebook, Skype, Zoom, WhatsApp, WeChat and whatever virtual communications their prospects have become accustomed to using.
  - Marketing can share their social media best practices.
  - Marketing can create social media or communications tool kits for sales.

On-demand availability: buyers expect to reach out seller at their own time using their preferred channels.

- Set up expectations for customer response time in texting, email or other forms of communications. Create dos and don'ts of 24/7 communications to avoid burn-out and communications fatigue. Make it part of onboarding and continuous training.
  - Marketing can break down content into snackable and digestible formats and incorporate into social media toolkits.
  - Marketing can work with sales to incorporate the kit as part of onboarding or continuous training.
  - Marketing can share best practices on communication frequency to avoid burnout.

Continueds

Continued

Sales trend	Proposed solution	Marketing functions
Omnipresent social media: social media is where you can find buyer information and also engage with them.	• It's increasingly vital for sales to be available via social media channels. The challenge is that social media tools are updated and refreshed frequently; Facebook often adds new features, LinkedIn incorporates new lead generation tools. Social media tools don't stay static. Sales need continuous education on new features.	• Marketing can leverage their social media agencies or their own social media expertise to get sales up-to-speed.
Analytics-based prospecting: use data and modeling to find prospects.	• To transfer data into actions, sales organizations need to have tools in place and possibly hire data analysts to conduct analysis. • A workflow and methodology for data-based prospecting needs to be established. Data correlation and analysis need to be optimized and reviewed on a regular basis.	• Marketing need to integrate their data with sales' CRM. • Marketing can work with sales to create workflows and dashboards. • Marketing can use lower priority prospects found, to email marketing nurture campaigns and deliver them back to sales when prospects are ready.
Multigenerational sales teams and customer teams: Baby Boomer, Generation X and Millennials are all part of the sales force.	• In addition to gaining vertical-specific expertise, salespeople also need to be aware of the behavioral differences and key characteristics of these generations. Build and incorporate essential tactics for working effectively with generational differences. • Sales organizations will also encounter the challenges of assimilating and training Millennials and organizing a cohesive sales organization encompassing three generations.	• Marketing can take the lead in conducting research and persona segmentation that considers appropriate generational differences, contributing insights to sales training.

Globalization of teams and customer base: buyers from MNC expect global and local support.

- When dealing with a global purchase committee that includes members from different countries, the sales team need to find the balance of global vs local or headquarters (HQ) vs geographies (geos).
- As if verticalization and multi-generational customers are not complicated enough, sales teams need to take into account cultural, social and language differences so that messaging is conveyed correctly and professionally.
- Marketing's support structure needs to align with the sales organization.
- Marketing can collaborate with local teams to adapt audience insights, value propositions and content for each region.

Use of analytics to gain learner insights: use analytics to monitor sales training and development.

- With digital, everything is trackable. Establish a process to monitor and track training downloads and usage. Create a process to gather feedback from the sales team through interviews and online surveys.
- Use advanced platforms and tools to integrate intuitive and user-friendly designs into training.
- Marketing can leverage content they create for sales training. Some content can also be used for sales to share with prospects or existing accounts.
- Data download and usage allow marketing to optimize and improve future content.

Emergence of integrated learning environments as a necessity: use the devices that salespeople use to drive just-in-time learning.

- Identify the learning channels for formal and informal training. Map editorial topics and content formats to these channels.
- Incorporate gamification to support role plays in a virtual world. Use technologies to enable crowd learning – the collaborative use of peer knowledge in real time. Optimize mobile learning and video usage.
- Sales can help marketing understand their learning habits. Marketing can help sales connect the dots by incorporating some how-to content into sales training plans and different learning tools.
- Marketing can use their creative resources to make training more engaging and effective (a picture is worth a thousand words).

▶ *continued from page 53*

Alana and I asked ourselves: 'Why is that? What is so hard about supporting sales as a marketing person?' Frankly, it shouldn't be that difficult, right? Sales and marketing work in the same company. We share the same business goals. We market and sell the same products. In some organizations, we even report to the same manager or belong to the same group. We should be on the same team. Well, the devil is in the detail.

Fundamentally, sales and marketing differ on:

- **Different department goals:** sales focus on revenue, while marketing focus on demand generation and brand recognition or both.

- **Different long-term and short-term priorities:** sales are in the trenches focusing on monthly and quarterly quotas, while marketing need to focus on mass brand awareness and facilitate prospects throughout the purchase funnel, which takes time beyond one month or one quarter.

- **Different resources and support allocation:** the sales process and methodology are more linear, while a customer's purchase cycle goes back and forth between top and the middle of the funnel before they make the final decision on a purchase. Sales resource allocation is based on sales processes, while marketing outreach tends to be channel-based or purchase journey-driven.

If these concerns and differences are not discussed and addressed between sales and marketing on a timely basis, the misalignment and friction will continue. As tension builds, frustration begins to simmer and then, no matter what marketers do, no effort is good enough.

Remember

Sales and marketing friction is derived from:

- different goals
- different priorities
- different approaches on resource and budget allocation

Here is the reality that we need to acknowledge: no matter how much we want to align, there will always be a level of misalignment due to fundamental differences in goals, priorities, and customer outreach approaches. Sales and marketing will never *fully* align due to differences in the time horizons of their goals. The key is to acknowledge the differences and take specific actions to find commonalities, using that as a way to minimize misalignments.

These are recommended steps to achieve synergy between marketing and sales that we will examine in this chapter:

- Find commonalities in misalignment.
- Focus on joint priorities and strategic accounts.
- Establish a service level agreement (SLA) with clear metrics.

Find commonalities in misalignment

If the sales team had their way, they would prefer marketing spend all their budget and resources only on the bottom of the purchase funnel. However, marketing's job is to cover the whole purchase funnel from brand awareness down to post-sales. It's hard to acquire new customers if marketers are not building awareness of products and services. Yet, it's very difficult to demonstrate how brand awareness 'helps the sale'. John Wanamaker, an accomplished merchant who built one of the first successful department stores in the US in the early 1900s, lamented, 'Half the money I spend on advertising is wasted; the trouble is, I don't know which half.' It's true – it's hard to directly tie awareness campaigns to a solid short-term return on investment (ROI) or even associate it with long-term growth.

For example: could you associate a purchase you made today with a commercial you were exposed to or a specific piece of content you consumed online as far back as four or six months ago? That exposure was just part of a mix of activities and touchpoints that ultimately led to a purchase. As you came closer to finalizing the decision, the content you engaged with around the time of the purchase, such as data sheets, competitive guides and product specifications, is likely to get most of the credit. Because business decision makers might mistakenly give too much weight to these 'bottom of the funnel' content pieces, it's easy to fall into the trap of re-allocating budget to something that you can measure and reducing budget for awareness-based campaigns that are hard to measure. Bear in mind, even though Wanamaker was not sure which half of his marketing was working, he still committed to run his campaigns aggressively and consistently. But note the key word: consistently.

With digital marketing, there is an abundance of trackable data. The problem is that we reach a point of data overload and analysis paralysis. There is an emerging trend of moving beyond the last-click model and embracing more comprehensive attribution models, for example 'non-last click' or 'time decay'. Take a look at the Attribution Modeling Overview published by Google, for example.[1] Until these models are widely adopted, we will continue to face the same issues – trying to identify which half of the marketing budget is working and which half is not.

Even with new attribution models, the results are only good for a single point in time. Think about this: Facebook ads may drive more traffic to a website than email campaigns this month. Next month, it may be the other way around because of a different call-to-action, discount or more interesting and engaging creative content. We need to constantly optimize our outreach and budget allocations, but that makes it hard to nail down a definitive value for portions of the marketing spend over time. Thus, back to Wanamaker's point: We are still unsure which half of marketing is not working because of constant optimization.

The truth is that marketing will need to take care of the whole purchase funnel, while sales focuses on the bottom of the funnel to qualify prospects and convert opportunities. It's here where the tension starts to build. Should the marketing team focus solely on investing in the bottom of the funnel to fully align with the sales team? That will not and should not happen. What we need is to find commonalities within misalignment. The opportunity here is to bring certain sales elements into marketing campaigns and create a healthy blend of lead generation in an environment that also raises awareness of the brand, allowing for broader reach. That requires a lot of brain-storming, planning and collaboration, and is certainly much harder to do than simple email pushes, social media posts, blog writing or even keyword-buys.

Here is a great example of finding commonalities within goal misalignment: when Alana was a Marketing Director for Oracle, one interesting programme she ran was an integrated effort that included sponsored events hosted by the *Wall Street Journal* and the CMO (Chief Marketing Officer) Council. Typically, the standard event sponsorship package includes banner ads, logo presence at the event venue, maybe a keynote or speaking opportunity, content within a programme guide and on the website, a booth or a 15-minute quick product introduction. It's more top of the funnel marketing outreach. However, these sponsorship elements weren't going to be sufficient to generate high-quality leads for her sales team. The challenge for Alana was how to find the commonalties to build top of the funnel awareness yet provide quality leads. Also, the product Oracle was looking to promote, Oracle CRM, was targeted at both sales and marketing teams. Alana's team decided it was worthwhile to build a bridge between those siloed teams. Thus, Alana worked with the sponsorship team to craft a series of one-day workshops, hosted in a handful of cities around the world. The attendees of the workshops had to include a sales and marketing pair from each organization – one salesperson and one marketing person joining forces to learn from each other and understand how technology can aid both parts of the organization in unique ways.

The workshops were designed to give value to the attendees; content was carefully crafted, instructors with highly credible backgrounds were hand-selected. Special attention was paid to the learning environment too: all workshops were hosted in universities or academic institutions, instead of hotels or business centres. And despite Oracle being a 'proud sponsor', there was actually very little infusion of Oracle CRM into any part of the day. It was imperative the attendees walked away feeling as if they better understood their sales or marketing counterpart and could form a better bond inside their organization for future growth.

Of course, there was more to it than that. Alana's team digested all of the dialogues from each session, taking away insights about how or why salespeople and marketers hit roadblocks. They took notes from discussions about the challenges of launching new technology or making financial decisions. These insights and comments were ultimately used to produce many pieces of content, all of which contributed to larger and broader ad campaigns – providing even greater scale and reach.

To create a customized sponsor element, such as Oracle's workshop, a number of key steps need to be considered:

- Brainstorm in advance and think of a unique way to add value not only to the event, but also your company. It's about creating a win–win.
- Coordinate with sales and marketing to find instructors or facilitators.
- Work with sales to invite existing account attendees and identify other prospects.
- Collaborate with the training and other team members to create workshop content.
- Craft promotional materials for sponsors and event managers to use (these can be in different formats).
- Prepare presenters with materials and provide on-site support.
- Consolidate and analyse feedback and insights for future editorial and content planning.
- Follow up post-event by sharing the content through marketing campaigns to generate additional leads.

It's multi-faceted and complex, yet it satisfies the needs of both marketing and sales, and provides a number of key benefits:

- The events provided warm leads from a marketer and salesperson that had recently formed a greater partnership inside their own organization.
- The content that was generated as a result of the workshops became evergreen content that could be utilized and syndicated for lead generation for the next six to twelve months.
- The sponsorship and promotion that came from WSJ and CMO Council not only provided air cover and awareness, but also third-party validation of the content.

This sponsorship could easily have been just awareness-based marketing, but Oracle found a way to create an angle, so sales could participate, and at the same time, turn leads into warm leads or even potential prospects. You don't need to do that for every sponsorship, but it's wise to identify two or three high-performing sponsorships and brainstorm interesting or creative ideas that will open more doors for sales team participation but are not too sales-oriented.

This type of customized sponsorship is not easy to scale, especially if you want to do it right. It also creates additional work for marketing managers. In general, marketing would prefer to take on the standard sponsorship package because it's easy and scalable. Event managers who manage more than ten events per year need to function fast and efficiently. Once an event is done, they need to move on to the next. This type of customization effort adds a lot of work for marketing managers who are already over-worked and stressed.

Focus on joint priorities

Although sales and marketing need to accomplish the same business objectives, their approaches to achieve them are likely to be very different. Thus, they have their own priorities for the year. Sales teams may identify new target accounts, optimize sales processes, implement new tools or accelerate sales cycles. Marketing teams may focus on product launches, website refresh, marketing automation upgrades, and so on. We both believe that aligning priorities is another key way of building a strong relationship between sales and marketing. The alignment on priorities will also guide and narrow the disparity in budget, resource and skillsets and address goal misalignment issues. Remember that you don't need to be aligned on every priority. I suggest that you focus on two or three priorities that sales and marketing can work on together. For example: the back-end integration of marketing automation and CRM, improving the quality of data and dashboards, targeting specific verticals and personas collectively, something as simple as agreeing to host a specific number of customers' events.

Google is famous not only for its search engine, but also for G-suite, Gmail, Google Maps, Google Trends, YouTube, autonomous cars and much more. Here is a twist of irony: as much as Google creates various products to enhance our digital and online experience, its sales and marketing teams still believe that face-to-face events are the best ways to create leads, convert prospects and grow business. But Google's event strategy does not validate an events-only marketing approach. Bear in mind, Google reaches out to its target audiences through integrated outreach, which combines both online and offline media. When you get people to show up at your events, you have a chance to show the magic; to share what you can offer and delight your audience with your brand. It gives sales a physical venue to mingle, network, share and understand the needs of people who attend (potential prospects). It's no surprise that Amazon, as big as they are online, started opening physical locations. It's the same approach: if shoppers wander into an Amazon store, there is a good chance they'll buy something.

Here are a couple of other examples from Alana's time at Google. She and her sales team prioritized events as joint initiatives to build awareness and grow prospects and leads:

- **Customer events:** Google Partners Accelerate debuted at Google's European headquarters in Dublin in 2014, and has grown bigger and better each year since.[2] This two-day event was tailored to 300 partners, showing off new product features, educating them on specialized techniques and industry trends and, most importantly, providing an opportunity for everyone to network. It was a chance for Google to build stronger connections with important customers, to learn more about each other, and to create a bit of excitement about future innovations. Sales teams were involved since key prospects and customers were invited. They were responsible for ensuring their clients' well-being, and they had a duty to follow up with the customers immediately afterwards. While the content on-stage was designed to show how Google products could assist in the overall growth and health of their business, teams went to great lengths to ensure all sessions were focused on education and learning versus anything that felt like a pitch. After all, it's about getting the right people in the room, providing good content and fodder for debate, and creating a space to help partnerships grow. All of which will ultimately aid in increasing the lifetime value of business, finding cross-sell and upsell opportunities, and great customer referrals.

- **Prospect events:** Half-day workshops or bootcamps are a great way to educate and establish credibility, especially today when technology moves faster than most people can adapt. This offers an opportunity to learn, to receive a hands-on introduction to the product and ask questions in front of experts which helps build trust and a deeper appreciation for the brand and product. For example, many businesses are aware of how powerful videos might be in building their brands, but it's difficult to know what and how to produce them. Workshops helped customers brainstorm specific ideas on the types of messaging and video content that would work for a certain brand, and they also helped in understanding the new technology that could produce videos quickly – without the need for an agency or production firm. Prospects could walk away in either instance with actionable next steps, working knowledge of the tools and strategies, and YouTube's sales team could better connect with prospects and speak to them in a common language. These types of events are truly sales enablement, as they help educate prospects to a level that allows for a bigger discussion on business growth.

Using events to grow prospects is nothing new. You can see similar tactics in other technology companies such as IBM, Microsoft, eBay, Salesforce.com, LinkedIn and Amazon. Well-established start-ups such as Airbnb, Shopify and others are also using the same tactics to network with existing customers and reach out to potential leads.

The key is to make it a *joint* priority between sales and marketing. Mike Weir, Vertical Director for Technology Industry at LinkedIn, told me that LinkedIn has a series of 'connect' events such as finance connect, sales connect, talent connect, even executive connect. These connect series events are imperative for sales and marketing. Marketing works on theme, venue, logistics, event elements and content to ensure a great on-site experience. The sales team provides feedback on the overall event directions and attendee invite list. Attendee acquisition is a joint responsibility between sales and marketing. For a big event, marketing concentrates on awareness-based and broad-based acquisition efforts, while salespeople focus on inviting specific customers and potential prospects. For the high-touch executive connect event, sales and marketing teams will nominate the names and sales executive will make a call on the final list.

Who develops the content for events and workshops? It can vary – but again, it's all about collaboration. In these two scenarios, most of the content was created by marketing and the sales enablement team. Sales would work diligently on all follow-up efforts and coordinate with marketing on post-event collateral. Everyone had a stake in the matter; all teams aligned on this joint initiative. Each took control of the areas that would make the most impact on their bottom line.

Creating a customized sponsorship opportunity for marketing to work closely with the sales team (Oracle sponsorship with the *Wall Street Journal*) and joint event planning (Google's Partner Accelerate) are just two examples of how to find commonalties within misalignments. It does not end there. Another way to find a joint priority is to align sales and marketing to target strategic prospects, which constitutes account-based sales and marketing. Sales identify the key accounts that they want to acquire. Marketing creates targeted and personalized campaigns and outreach that tailor to those accounts. Marketing also works with sales on account-based content creations and personalized value propositions based on account's firmographics and technographics. Firmographic data refers to attributes about the company, while technographics relate to the potential accounts' technology and organizational environment. Winning accounts is the common goal.

Establish a service level agreement with clear metrics

Hubspot publishes *State of the Inbound*, an annual survey of the latest sales and marketing challenges that businesses are facing. In 2017 *State of the Inbound* surveyed 6,399 professionals in 141 countries. And one of the key questions was, 'How would you characterize your company's sales and marketing relationship?' The response showed 44 per cent of respondents indicated that sales and marketing are *generally* aligned, while only 22 per cent indicated that they are *tightly* aligned. The definition of tightly aligned is that they have a formal SLA in place between the two groups. An SLA is a documentation (AKA a contract) between sales and marketing to identify roles and responsibilities as well commitments to deliverables within a certain timeframe. To ensure sales support is on marketing's radar and vice versa, it's essential to set up an SLA. Both parties need to agree on who will deliver what and when. In some cases, it's necessary to call out not just initiatives and deliverables, but also the success measurements. Set expectations upfront and communicate them clearly to all parties.

On an interesting note: the *State of the Inbound* 2017 survey also found that, among the companies with tight sales/marketing alignment and an SLA, sales teams ranked the marketing-sourced leads higher than the sales-sourced leads. When sales and marketing work closely together, the quality of marketing leads improves.

There are times when you will need to work outside the remit of this agreement. For example, if a company's sales are in decline and the position is precarious, that company may turn to marketing to see what new tactics can be deployed. Marketing should support this request even though it's out of the SLA. Dire situations call for adjustments from everyone, and marketing may need to run a last-minute campaign, shift budget around to win a specific account, or implement an unexpected game plan.

Marketing has the data to understand the company's overall prospects. There will be times when you may need to throw an SLA out the window and make necessary changes in marketing to support sales when the revenue is not going in the right direction. Both sales and marketing are working together to close the right kind of deals aligned with the company's objectives.

SLA example: agree on lead definition

Ask any salespeople what is the number one request they want from marketing. Ten out of ten sales teams will tell you it is to provide them with high-quality leads. Quality of leads has always been a contentious topic and a major contributor to the constant battle between marketing and sales teams. It's important for both teams to define what makes a high-quality sales lead.

Remember

Benefits of a clearly defined high-quality sales lead:

- avoids confusion between sales and marketing teams
- guides marketing's demand generation strategy and execution
- establishes a common understanding of lead characteristics
- drives tool integration between sales and marketing
- unifies dashboards and reports

William Wickey, Head of Content and Media Strategy at LeadGenius, explains how their marketing and sales teams agreed on the different stages of leads. This ensures that there is no debate on how to move leads further through the funnel:

Pre-qualified lead:	Inbound and outbound leads that fit the ideal customer profile (ICP)
Marketing qualified lead (MQL):	Pre-qualified + requests demo ('hand-raisers')
Sales accepted lead (SAL):	MQL criteria is validated by sales reps
Prospect:	SAL + completed ICP calibration (qualifying process specific to LeadGenius. Equivalent to SQL)
Demo scheduled:	Prospect agrees to a demo presentation
Evaluation:	Prospect has completed demo
Proposal:	Prospect has been sent contract
Committed:	Prospect has signed contract and has been sent payment link
Closed won:	Paying customer

The lead definitions are simple, clear and action-driven. So something as objective as clicking on a 'Request a demo' button on their website can be used to track the numbers of marketing qualified leads (MQLs). To define the leads, Wickey stresses that marketing need to understand the sales processes, which echoes my point in 'Pre-requisites for marketers to support sales'. Then, marketing can work backward to arrive at more accurate lead goals and budget projections. Obviously, the sales team also have their own lead goals in mind. From there, sales and marketing can meet to hash out the differences and reach an SLA.

LeadGenius offers another valuable practice: the SLA should not just be a static documentation of roles and responsibilities, jointly agreed lead goals and definitions of leads. It's also important that this SLA ultimately corresponds to fields and data in your marketing automation system (MAS) or CRM.

The next phase is to define the shared reporting dashboard. You need to develop a highly visible and easily accessible dashboard that is tracking all shared KPIs. You don't want confusion or disagreement when reporting in the future. Too often, marketing and sales teams agree on metrics, only to find out later that they are unintentionally 'keeping two sets of books'. For example, marketing may track new leads in Marketo then synchronize them with Salesforce. com where sales can use them. If the marketing team discovers that lead stage activity is not feeding back to Marketo the right way and skewing their numbers, a shared dashboard and agreed upon reports from the start mitigates this.

William suggested taking into account a number of criteria to define a high quality of lead:

3.1

- **Depth:** A lead is not a single data point. It's not a name or phone number. It's a cluster of relevant information, which includes demographics, firmographics, buying signals, contact information and qualified activity such as an online form submission.

- **Accuracy:** It is important to review data acquired through the lead generation process to make sure the information is accurate and applicable. Verifying the data allows your sales team to allocate time and resources to prospects with the highest probability of being receptive to your message.

- **Reliability:** This is about the process of gathering feedback from sales to improve the quality of the leads. Accurate information won't stay that way for long. Employees are hired and fired. Companies are merged or acquired. 'Some industries have as high as a 6.5 per cent monthly contact decay rate. This means that at the end of the year half of the contacts in their CRM could be inaccurate.'

- **Fitness:** This is a quality versus quantity discussion. Marketing are pressured to rack up MQLs that have indicated interest in your products or services but were not ready for a sales meeting or to buy. High-volume leads don't equate to more deals. Hitting the MQL goal doesn't mean the sales team will be pleased. It's important to focus on the conversion ratio. For example: fifty MQLs delivering ten sales are better than a hundred MQLs delivering five sales.[3]

- Although marketing has a goal on MQLs, the quality matters.

Lead definitions and sales processes differ for every company based on industry, product, company size, target buyers, etc. The key is consistency in tracking, pipeline definitions and conversion calculations. With that in place, you can effectively manage leads and predict deal closure rates. Clearly defining sales lifecycle stages is the key to moving leads smoothly through the purchasing funnel and building good workflows.

Remember

Here is the process that you can follow to address lead definitions and lead goals with your sales team:

- Understand the sales process.
- Agree to lead definitions at different stages of the sales process.
- Agree to lead goals and budget.
- Establish an SLA.
- Tie SLA to data and fields from MAS and CRM.
- Set joint dashboards (agree on the data sources).

Marketing and sales working to improve the lead process

In addition to the debate over lead quality, another contentious point is how to accurately measure the impact of lead generation. Lead generation impacts whether or not salespeople follow up on the marketing leads. And, if they do, can marketing tie the signed contract back to their leads? For example, when Alana was Director of Advertising at Oracle, her team supported a massive global sales organization and had the challenge of comprehending a complex ecosystem of lead routing and follow-through as well as ensuring her team measured the success of her lead generation efforts.

Her marketing team wasn't explicitly accountable for demonstrating that whitepaper registrations directly converted into net-new customers, but she was responsible for showing the impact of her efforts. Millions of dollars were spent on content syndication for the purpose of generating a large volume of high-quality leads for sales, and it was imperative she knew whether or not those dollars were having a positive impact on the business.

She ensured that a smooth lead-collection and hand-off process was in place: content distribution methods were expansive and efficient, assets were labelled clearly, landing pages were tagged, registration forms were available in multiple form factors on many types of devices, and it was easy to identify which content and distribution efforts yielded the greatest number of leads. Quantity wasn't an issue, per se.

Quality, on the other hand, was a mystery. Due to the complexity of the lead-routing infrastructure, her marketing team could only assess quality by the accuracy of the information that came through the registration form. In other words, her team would validate registration forms containing full names, business organizations, business email addresses and other contact information. This was the closest measurement of quality the team could glean. But this validation was not enough to prove the ROI or quality of leads. Without an effective means of reporting on quality and deal rate, she would run the risk of marketing dollars being redirected to other programmes.

This is an all too common situation. Marketing struggles to measure impact and senior leaders make the decision to scale down efforts, with budgets left to only those few instances where a clear conversion rate can be measured or for qualitative efforts that 'sales can't live without'. Alana took the challenge head-on. She explained her needs to the sales team, started a dialogue, established relationships and built a process to measure leads deeper in the funnel and optimize her efforts toward a better definition of quality.

When sales and marketing started talking, they discovered that there were gaps in communications and processes. For example, she educated her sales counterparts on how to better identify marketing leads rather than other leads in the database, using unique tagging and labelling. She also rallied several sales managers to help her raise awareness of marketing leads to the rest of the sales organization. This led to salespeople being better able to identify a marketing lead, and led them to follow up accordingly. Because she knew that the leads were being acted on, she could easily follow up and get feedback from sales regarding the quality of these leads. With that feedback, she was able to measure the quality of her leads and track conversions over time.

It was not easy. It took months of working with sales leaders and reps to understand exactly what parts of the process were broken. There's no waving of a magic wand – just a comprehensive review from both parties and many 'dumb questions' that need to be worked through in order to find the best ways to move forward. Again, this takes commitment from both parties and a trusted environment that allows for open dialogue.

Alana acknowledges that it was a great deal of manual work, especially when the systems were not talking to each other. Even when the systems were connected, sales may not have updated the information in CRM, and she would still need to reach out to individual salespeople to get updates.

Unless tools and processes are kept up-to-date, proving the impact of lead generation, like data analytics, requires work, time and effort. At the same time, there is also a lead-lag effect. What if a great lead expressed a strong interest in talking to the sales team (this lead can be counted in quantity) but, since it may take quite a while to close any related sale, evaluating the quality of the lead won't be possible until later? This lag effect adds to the challenges of proving the ROI of lead generation.

By talking to Alana, I create a process that you can also follow to address the lead process:

- Create relevant content with a seamless user interface and a responsive registration form.
- Validate the lead's contact information.
- Confirm that marketing processes dovetail with sales and lead routing processes.
- Label and/or tag everything clearly (some marketing automation tools have built-in intelligence, so you may not need to do manual labelling and tagging).
- Educate sales on how to use their marketing leads effectively.
- Rally sales managers to spread the word.
- Use CRM to monitor activity and following up with sales.
- Quantify the conversion rate results.

Solicit sales feedback and comments

The best method to truly get feedback is simply to live in their shoes. Marketing can shadow a salesperson for a focused view into a day in the life of a rep – to see first-hand how a rep engages with customers, where they find and manage their leads, how they communicate the product benefits and value, and how they handle tough objections. Marketers should shadow both highly skilled and more junior sales team members to see the tools each rep uses along the way. It gives marketers valuable insight into the reality of the business. While it may seem intrusive, if the sales reps understand the reasoning behind the shadowing and trust the motives behind this feedback collection process they will be open to sharing even more pain points.

If this approach isn't feasible, or if more data is desired, sales should provide marketing with feedback through surveys or focus groups – all with the collaboration of marketing from the onset. This is important to reiterate: there's a risk that sales will simply ask for more events, more leads and more presentation support. These asks shouldn't be underrated, but they're short-term asks and do not expose the true areas of future partnership for sales enablement efforts.

Questions for surveys or focus groups could include:

- What are the last five sales pitch presentations you used?
- What are the top questions you get asked about key competitors?
- How do you stay current on the company's product offerings?
- Where do you find and track high-potential opportunities (follow up: how do you know if an opportunity is high-potential)?
- How many interactions do you have with a client before you close a deal?
- When you weren't able to close a deal, what were the reasons?
- How easy is it to explain our products to a prospect? What references or material do you use to help?

This feedback gives marketing an understanding of:

- how well their reps know the product
- what pitch templates and strategies work best
- how reps communicate the value of the offering, especially compared to the competition
- how much time reps spend sourcing, tagging, updating and dismissing leads
- whether reps spend any time crafting external messages or other collateral

Responses to these questions will illuminate all the different tactics and strategies that marketing can deploy. Comments like 'Marketing's leads are rubbish', or 'Marketing needs to pay for more events', or 'Sales reps are getting hammered by the competition' are not constructive to further improve the relationship. It would be great to receive specific feedback that relates to processes, tools, communications, content, skillsets or organization structures. It will give marketing ideas on what needs to be improved. Feedback is only useful if the receiver can clearly identify realistic areas for improvement.

It's a great deal of work to support sales

Have you noticed a trend in this chapter? Supporting sales as a marketer is difficult work, and it's even more difficult to do it right. At Oracle the efforts to find a way to customize a sponsorship opportunity that turned leads to potential prospects during a one-day workshop was a great example of the amount of work required to enable sales properly. Aligning priorities for event planning in order to create a seamless experience that encouraged customers and partners to network was also a tremendous endeavour.

The key question is not what to do. I believe that marketers, in general, know what needs to be done. It's not about doing the right thing, it's about doing things right, which takes time and effort. Sales will need to meet marketing half way to support their efforts.

Marketers understand that salespeople are their allies and they want to prove their worth. In order to do that, marketers need to seek out ways to stay close to the sales teams and their activities. That isn't enough, though. Sales teams owe their marketing teams feedback and input. They need to do more than just 'take' from the strategies – they also need to give back. It's about working together to engage, communicate and optimize. It's a case of 'help me to help you'.

In his book *Achieve Sales Excellence*, Howard Stevens set out the Seven Rules of the Customers: 'You must be personally accountable for our results.'[4] At the end of the day, it's not about sales or marketing. It's about taking responsibility for 'serving customers' personally. The foremost concern of salespeople, says Stevens, 'is that the customer achieves the best solutions, the results that they expected and paid for'. It reminds me of my experiences at the Apple store and Nordstrom. The salespeople take their responsibilities personally. That's the mentality needed to effectively work with the sales team.

What you can do

1 List three potential initiatives that you can do to find 'commonalities in misalignment'.

2 Shadow your salespeople one day or take them out for lunch or a cup of coffee and get to know them better.

3 Start having conversations about:

- the definition of a high-quality sales lead

- the ROI of lead generation

- anything you want to talk to your sales team about – the topic isn't as important as having an ongoing conversation

Notes

1 Google. Attribution modeling overview. https://support.google.com/analytics/answer/1662518?hl=en

2 See Google Partners Accelerate overview video. https://youtu.be/d3s-Qqs8-bU

3 William Wickey. The 4 pillars of lead quality: What is a high quality sales lead? Mobile Marketing Match, 14 August 2016. https://mobilemarketingwatch.com/the-4-pillars-of-lead-quality-what-is-a-high-quality-sales-lead-66360

4 Bill Hart. 7 rules your customers expect you to follow. 28 September 2017. http://info.billhartbizgrowth.com/7-rules-of-the-customer

Branding and messaging also apply to sales   04

A brand is a result, not a tactic.
LUCAS CONLEY, FAST COMPANY

Branding is the art of aligning what you want people to think about your company with what people actually do think about your company. And vice versa.
JAY BAER, AUTHOR OF *TALK TRIGGERS*

When I started in marketing several years ago, I was told by my manager at that time that the same messaging needs to reach the same customers at least seven times before it will stick. In marketing, messaging refers to how we articulate our brand and product positioning in the market place. Positioning refers to why customers should use our products instead of competitors, and our product promise. Messaging is what we should say about our company, brand and products. Marketing messaging provides direction to content creators on copywriting so that similar talking points can be used consistently across different channels, while the brand guide offers the guardrails for the overall look and feel. For a brand to stick in a prospect's mind, consistency is the key.

My husband, Michael, owns a huge amount of music. He listens to different genres from classical, opera, jazz and rock to underground and alternative. He even keeps up with hip-hop because our sons frequently share their playlists with us. Even when he hears a song or a piece of classical music that he doesn't know, he can often correctly identify the singer, group, or composer. If he turns out to be wrong about an educated guess, he can explain why he came up with his answers. He explains that each singer or composer has a certain style.

If you listen carefully, you can hear that there's a consistency to the way most artists use their favourite techniques or arrangements.

While I don't have his broad knowledge or have his ear to hear the distinctions between different singing or composing techniques, I completely understand his point about the consistency of styles. That's was exactly the point my first marketing manager was making. Consistent messaging for a brand over a long period of time fosters the brand recognition that may pay dividends when a potential customer has a relevant need. To use another metaphor, marketing is like gardening. You need to nurture leads and, even though you apply consistent attention to them, some will wither while others will mature and can then be harvested and handed off to sales. You need to be consistent in the full spectrum of marketing and sales activities related to the brand, from copywriting, creative, reach and frequency to sales engagements. After all, sales and marketing are a continuum that needs to be well planned and properly facilitated to be effective.

Consistency is key

Consistency does not mean communicating the same thing in every channel every day. As brands, you can communicate different topics and use different creative layouts, but certain design or communications rules stay intact so that your customers instantly make the association with your brand when they see your ads or marketing messages. That unique differentiator can be conveyed in many different ways: taglines, spokespersons, logos, colours, sounds, slogans, images, tone and manner, or a combination of these.

When I see the first five seconds of some TV commercials, certain brands will quickly come to mind. The brand's DNA or style of communication is imprinted deeply into the creative and message development. I can always tell when a Target commercial is playing on TV. Target is one of the largest discount retail stores in the United States. Their logo is a bright red and white bullseye with three rings. They don't usually show the logo until the end of the commercials, but they creatively use the bullseye shape as a prop or as part of the story. And the colours of red and white are prominently displayed. Viewers can easily pick up subtle hints that they are watching a Target commercial. Another great example is Apple. Not only do their commercials adhere to strict style guidelines, co-marketing materials with different telecommunications providers also retain the same qualities, so they are also instantly recognizable as 'Apple'. Even with new content from their partners, I am able to identify the brand based on that subtle consistency of style that my husband was talking about. I am sure that you can name several brands with a unique look and feel to their TV commercials or marketing materials that always brings their brand immediately to your awareness. Look at Conley's and Baer's quotes at the beginning of this chapter: the way these companies execute their branding strategies clearly and vividly communicates who they are as if their brands have distinctive personalities and styles.

Consistency also means that you need be present on a regular basis. It doesn't mean that you have to be on all marketing channels all the time. There are some channels that require consistent presence, while some don't. If you blog once a week, you blog once a week. If you are committed to placing content on social media channels two to five times a week, then, make an effort to publish two to five times a week. Product launches, paid campaigns or sponsorships are not on a regular cadence, but the highlights and announcements of these efforts can certainly be part of consistent blog and social media outreach.

However, it's important that the quantity of output does not outpace your ability to provide relevant content with consistent quality. You need to ask yourself: Do we have something new or useful to share? Is our content relevant to our customers? Do not blog for the sake of blogging. Do not use social media for the sake of social media. Do not be consistent for the sake of being consistent.

Remember

To be consistent or not to be consistent, that is the question. Although marketers need to make that decision, the ultimate goal is to define an ideal customer experience that your team wants to convey. If you use a specific creative concept or write in a certain style, does that communicate the brand consistency that you are looking for? It's about understanding what your brand represents and how your customers perceive the products.

It's indeed an *art* of aligning what you want people to think about your company with what people actually think about your company. Easy to say, but hard to accomplish, which is why establishing a brand guide is so important.

The catalyst for consistent brand and messaging

The way that brands or products are presented or communicated will make an impression on potential customers. Typically, this is due to the creative use of multiple marketing elements:

4.1

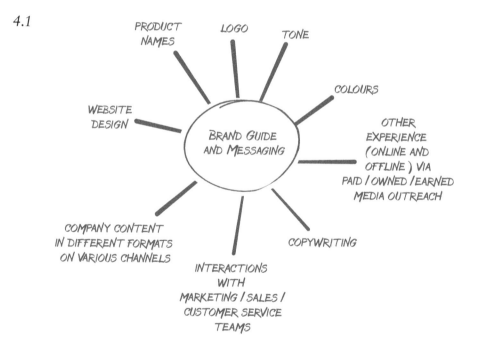

To create the desired impressions, these elements cannot be used randomly, and need to be connected in some manner to deliver a brand continuum. It needs to be designed and carefully thought through.

Remember

A crisp brand guide and clear product messaging framework should steer the way.

- Brand guide: define the brand's look and feel, and tone and manner.
- Messaging framework: explain the product's unique value propositions.

Brand and messaging framework's role in sales

Although brand guides and messaging frameworks serve as the foundation for marketing communications, they are also source and reference documents for the sales teams. Both documents can apply to sales onboarding, training and content to facilitate sales processes or be used to plan customer conversations and meetings.

Brand guide

Every company, small or large, should have a brand guide. It can be as simple as setting up general rules on logo, colour and typography usage. It can be as detailed as the size and placement of logos on different media platforms and guidance on colour palettes and different typefaces. For global enterprises, the guide will also provide specifics on what *not* to do, since so many people and agencies around the world use the brand guide. On the surface, the purpose of a brand guide is to offer the rules and guidance for logo and font usage and creative development for marketing campaigns. The true essence of a brand is to shape both the look and feel, and the tone and manner so that your customers can identify your company and brand when they see your content.

In addition to providing guidance for internal team members and agencies, some global enterprises also need to provide guidelines for many different partners they work with worldwide. I mentioned Apple at the beginning of this chapter. The company goes the extra mile to protect their brands and ensure that they won't be diluted as part of co-branding or co-marketing efforts.

It gets even more complicated with technologies. With the rise of 2D and 3D digital content, some brand guides have added new categories such as motion, movement, imagery, icon, choreography and shapes of user interfaces. The best example of digital content guidance is Google's Material Design website.[1] This online brand guide was introduced to help designers and developers embrace an expanding, multi-device and multi-screen world. Marketers are not used to thinking about marketing communications in 2D or 3D formats. When you add another dimension, there are many more elements that you need to take into account to ensure the brand consistency. Sometimes, I feel that I need to think like a user-interface designer, a film-maker or an interior designer to fully grasp the additional elements that will need to be included in the brand guide for the new 3D era. Ultimately, no matter the format or media outlet, the brand guide provides the rules to shape the design and experience.

Some brand guides will also include the company's vision, product information and brand persona (personality). A brand persona is different from a buyer persona. Brands are personified with a set of human characteristics to help bring focus to 2D/3D content designers. A buyer persona is a semi-fictional representation of your ideal customer based on market research and real data about your existing customers. Both have their place in marketing and sales communications.

Here are two examples of brand personas. Jo Berrington, Marketing Director of Yotel, an affordable luxury hotel group based in London with presence in New York, Boston, Amsterdam, Singapore, Paris and San Francisco, created Yotel's brand guide when the company was formed. She made sure whoever is using the brand guide also understands the brand's persona and embeds the personalities into creative development and campaign creation. Yotel's personality can be described in five words, a combination of rational and emotional values:

- smart
- inspiring
- honest
- efficient
- empathetic

Brian Fravel was Intel's VP of Marketing and brand steward for many years. He led Intel's master logo rebranding in 2006, which included creating and updating its brand guides. His team crafted Intel's personality using four words:

- bold
- optimistic
- passionate
- unexpected

Brand personas help designers, content creators and writers craft new creative concepts, select specific words and source appropriate images. They ensure that the finished content they conceive is on brand.

Usage of the brand guide in sales content

The purchase journey from marketing to sales is a continuum. Customers may go back and forth between sales and marketing personnel or materials, but the overall experience should stay the same. The content they receive from either sales or marketing should have the same look and feel with the same tone and manner or similar writing or communications style. The design of conference booths should be based on the same style guide as a company's website to provide customers with a similar experience and increase their brand awareness. To ensure consistency and make it easy for the sales teams, marketing can create branded templates for email, presentations and other forms of content, such as customer testimonials, solutions briefs, etc. In some companies, sales training and development must also conform to the rules of the brand guide. My general rule of thumb: use the guide for internal training development as well as external engagements.

The sales teams is the brand

A brand is much more than some rules applied to sales processes and communications. In some companies, the brand guide is expanded to cover the dress code (think of airline flight attendants' uniforms), office or store design including interior colours and furniture selection (think of fast-food franchises), and making sure the brand persona is considered when recruiting talent. At a macro level, the nirvana of a brand is achieved when its essence and its promise are woven into every aspect of a company, from corporate culture, employees' actions, hiring and recruiting down to the new employee handbook and sales orientation.

Sales teams are the frontline interface of a brand. Marketing creates the brand guide, but sales reps, account managers, customer service and support teams all shape the customer experience and bring brand promises to life. While a brand guide is written to reflect who you are and what you stand for, it does not define who you are, but it helps to display it. The reinforcement of brand and its value, occasionally, is complicated by how sales teams are incentivized. 'Compassionate brands don't reward greed,' says Mark Di Somma. 'Exciting brands don't accept complacency.'[2] Sales wins are important, but it's also important to be clear on how the sales team goes about it. For complex sales, people *are* the brand and the unique differentiator.

Though the brand guide may be made by marketing, it is critical for sales to be meaningful contributors and buy in to it, and it needs to be required reading for all salespeople. At most companies, the brand guidelines are not as widely distributed as they should be. They are mostly distributed to the marketing group and their contractors, and rarely makes it to sales and their partners.

Remember

Salespeople should be familiar with the brand guides so that they know how to write social media posts, select proper images or use logos and fonts properly. Most importantly, salespeople should understand the brand persona; they are the brand ambassadors.

Messaging framework

All of us have experienced sleepless nights. Before the iPhone was launched and Netflix began streaming in 2007, what did we do when we couldn't sleep? Well, some of us would turn on the TV in the hope of finding something diverting. Unfortunately, very late nights and early morning TV channels were filled with infomercials. I would change the channel whenever I saw one. Obviously, whoever was buying the time slots had some success, though, otherwise we would not have seen so many of them. Everyone I talked to agreed that these infomercials are lame, but somehow, many of us made purchases of one or another of those items. Remember the popular and original blue Snuggie blanket? I bought one.

Here are several reasons why infomercials have the magic to close sales, despite being disliked by so many:

- Clear product message and user benefits (*Saves you time. Easy cleaning*)
- Persuasive show-and-tell (*Look how easy it is to install*)
- Discounted pricing and small monthly instalments (*Only $9.99 a month for three months!*)
- Urgent call to action (*Limited time offer! Call now!*)

The keys are a clear product message and user benefits. They dramatize the pain points and frustration, then use show-and-tell to explain how the product will solve our issues. Immediately after that, they mention several superb user benefits and repeat them several times with urgent calls-to-action to buy before it's too late. Every infomercial follows the same script and sales process.

Unlike infomercials, it's not easy to identify crisp product messages and user benefits in B2B selling. B2B platforms or products usually have numerous product features and end-user benefits that may vary in value, based on the use case or the audience.

As marketers or salespeople, we need to prioritize product features and benefits and use short, concise statements to convey the awesomeness of our products. That's where a messaging framework comes into play.

It's interesting that sales and marketing often focus on content, but we sometimes neglect messaging. The reality is that the development of messaging is not exciting and requires a lot of ground work to create a solid framework. Yet, it's crucial to guide everything related to marketing, from content creation, website design, copy writing and brief writing to the calls-to-action of different content pieces. A messaging framework can also guide sales tele-scripts, pitches and customer meeting planning.

Remember

Messaging drives marketing and sales activities and streamlines communication so that the content prospects see on your website translates well into demos and sales conversations.

The key is to craft a message that is relevant to something your prospects care deeply about: themselves.

Ownership of a messaging framework

In general, messaging is owned by marketing, but it can also be led by product marketing in a product group or a business unit. It doesn't matter who owns it, as long as someone is able to convert product features to user benefits in plain English and in a way that resonates with the target audience. Then, marketers can make the user benefits a source for copywriting and marketing communications, while sales can use them as a source to prepare for conversations and meetings with prospects and customers.

Identify key messaging

Messaging needs to meet two criteria:

- identify the uniqueness of your products
- be relevant to your customers

Erik Peterson, author of *The Three Value Conversations*, calls it the 'Value Wedge'.[3] It's a sweet spot that meets your prospects' needs and differentiate your offerings. To do that, you will need to understand

your product features, customer pain points and competitors' offerings. Marketing, sales and product managers need to work together
to identify key messages. The best way to do that is to start a brain-
storming session. As a team, think through your company's products,
services, processes and organization and write down anything that
differentiates you from your competitors or resonates with existing
customers. List *all* of the product features.

Sometimes, small features can become the biggest selling points.
You just never know. Most messaging for automobiles focuses on
how embedded technologies make drivers' commute productive,
features that recognize your voice and connect with your phone
seamlessly, or even the performance of going from 0 to 65 miles per
hour in three seconds. To me, it's a little feature like seat comfort.
If my body can just fit into that car seat comfortably, it becomes a
major decision point when I shop for a car. Apparently, I was not the
only one commenting on seat comfort. Several friends commented
how comfortable Lexus' seats are. This small feature became one of
my key decisions to buy a Lexus. Another example: Les Schwab, a car
tyre store in the US, offers complimentary services – wheels and even
car maintenance. One small feature Schwab offers is that anyone,
regardless of whether he or she purchased from the store, can call in
any time and have the air pressure of their tyres checked and adjusted
for free. This is a fairly trivial feature but one that has helped them to
achieve significant brand awareness and customer loyalty.

Peterson recommends that you list all the features and then assign
numeric values to them based on the following criteria, to help you
quickly differentiate your products and services:

- Score it as 2.
- If it's something that others have, but you can prove that your
  company does it better, score it as 1.
- If it's something that competitors can do about as well, score it as 0.

Get rid of the zeros, because they offers no differentiation. Focus
on the 2s and 1s. To keep your message crisp and your conversation clear, Peterson suggests identifying the three most important
messages as your talking points.

Peterson quotes an article by Kurt Carlson from Georgetown University and Suzanne Shu from UCLA: 'They discovered that if customers know that the message is coming from a source with a persuasive motive, then the optimal number of positive claims is three.' It's interesting that the messaging frameworks I have worked on at Intel also followed this 'rule of three'.

Once you have identified your top three 'Value Wedge' points, you can prioritize and map them to customers' existing challenges. For outbound marketing communications, it's essential to focus on addressing customers' known and existing challenges. Since their pain points will cause them to actively search for solutions, this will make it likely that your offerings appear as they search.

Lead generation marketing efforts need to focus on solving customers' known challenges with unique positioning and value propositions that differentiate your products and company.

The approach needs to change when prospects become sales qualified leads. The sales team can also continue to carry on the conversation of solving a prospect's known issues. However, a salespeople's value-add increases dramatically when they can find needs that the prospects have not thought about nor considered. Peterson called these 'unconsidered needs'. According to Daniel Pink, author of *To Sell is Human*, salespeople need to rely on the ability to find problems, rather than just solve problems. 'Your products and services are far more valuable when you can tell buyers something they didn't know about a problem or of a missed opportunity that they didn't know they had.'

Messaging framework approach

If you Google 'messaging framework', you will get hundreds of templates and approaches; all roads lead to Rome. You need to find one that works for you and your team. In general, messaging is product-driven. Your sales methodology can be solutions-based. But the messaging framework should be grounded on products. Here is how you tie product messaging to a solution-based sales approach: use product features to identify user benefits, then tie those user benefits to situations faced by your customers. Ultimately, a solution-based approach needs to tie to what the sales team will sell and what customers want to buy.

EXISTING → VALUE → POSITIONING → MESSAGING → PROOF
CHALLENGES ← PROPOSITION ← POSITIONING ← MESSAGING ← POINTS

- **Existing challenges:** What are your customer's pain points and challenges?
- **Value proposition:** How is your product differentiated in the market place? How does your product compare to that of your competitors?
- **Positioning:** What is your product's promise? Why should customers use your product instead of your competitors'?
- **Messaging:** How can we solve customer pain points and challenges?
- **Proof points:** What product features and claims substantiate the key messaging?

4.3

UNCONSIDERED NEEDS → MESSAGING → PROOF POINTS

- **Customers' unconsidered needs:** What are the unknown, undervalued, or unmet challenges that your prospects and customers are not even thinking about?
- **Messaging:** What are our key talking points to meet customers' unconsidered needs that will create unconsidered value opportunity?
- **Proof points:** What product features and claims substantiate the key messages?

Messaging between sales and marketing will not always align 100 per cent. Marketing messaging needs to be consistent from channel to channel. The copywriting, creative and calls-to-action can change according to different content topics, but brand, value proposition, positioning and messaging should stay intact. The key is to keep the messaging crisp, limited and focused. Salespeople should be aware of the messaging framework and make an effort to use it whenever possible. However, marketing need to understand that sales will customize their talking points based on when and with whom they talk. This is especially true in an account-based approach.

In enterprises, a messaging framework requires external marketing research from customers, competitive product analysis and internal feedback from management and subject matter experts. There are usually numerous rounds of discussions and meetings required to finalize the framework for large and mid-size companies. It may be an easier exercise for a smaller company with fewer people, but you still need to go through the same analysis.

Because a messaging framework needs to get buy-in from internal stakeholders (subject matter experts, product marketing managers, legal and more), it usually can't be changed continuously. Again, this comes back to consistency. The messaging stays the same, but you can pick and choose what messaging and proof points to use for different audiences. In addition, it's acceptable to test new messaging ideas in the field or change the messaging when new products are launched. If you want to build that long-term consistent perception about your products and company, you need to be careful about what positioning needs to stay the same and what needs to be modified. It's about balance. It also comes down to your product roadmap and the features that will be added over time.

Message/customer fit

Myk Pono, marketing and product growth consultant, defined messaging in this way:

> We all know about product/market fit, which is essentially finding suffi-
> cient demand for your product in a big or growing market. What we
> often forget is getting to product/market fit means getting to message/
> customer fit as well. Convincing early customers to buy is essentially

testing not only how a product solves a customer's needs, but also how its value is communicated.[4]

Although sales may personalize user-benefits for different personas, the messaging and proof points stay the same. For example: the key messaging is 'Run your business with ease.' Salespeople can position their product to IT managers as 'easy to install' and 'smooth migration', while the same product could be positioned to the VP of sales as 'access monitor dashboard anytime and anywhere with ease'. Even though the talking points are different, have you noticed that it's all grounded on the core of 'with ease'?

The essence of messaging should also be woven into website content and communications materials including ads, PR, blogs, email and more. By consuming the information, prospects formulate their perceptions about your brand and products before they are qualified by marketing and inside sales.

Remember

To maintain that consistency, brand guidelines and messaging also need to be part of sales training, materials and collateral for sales processes. When salespeople dig hard to find unconsidered needs or focus on specific accounts, marketing can provide personalized and customized content to support their targeted efforts.

In addition to addressing unconsidered needs, messaging can also be mapped to sales processes or stages. Instead of starting with messaging, marketers can work with sales enablement to identify needed content and information to address unconsidered needs to complement sales tactics. Once you have identified the list, determine which content to adopt as is, which to modify and what new materials need to be created. If you modify or create new content, you can use the messaging framework as a source document to support your efforts.

In addition, most sales teams also have clear sales playbooks. Sales playbooks describe in detail such things as sales pitches, competitive landscapes, product differentiation, target customer profiles, product offerings and descriptions, battle cards and customer success stories.

4.4

Key elements of a sales playbook:

- product or solution description
- competitive intelligence and analysis
- customer challenges
- responses to customers challenges
- value proposition
- elevator pitch
- messaging framework
- proof points
- approach plan
- conversation starters
- deal characteristics
- buyers' roles and lines of business
- customer wins
- client presentation examples
- offering overview and datasheet
- buying factors
- relevant marketing content as pass-through
- and more…

Relevant messaging must be incorporated into sales playbooks to deliver coherent and consistent communications.

Other types of messaging

The messaging framework I've discussed is product-based and can apply to both sales and marketing. There are other types of messaging that have their place.

- **Thought leadership messaging:** Marketing messaging, not related to products or services, is more visionary and aspirational. This type of messaging is likely to serve marketing campaigns that focus on corporate social responsibilities for the well-being of society, innovations to create a better future for mankind, or enablement of advanced technologies and ecosystems. Although its tie to sales is less direct, it is a great talking point with corporate level executives and certainly helps build and reinforce the brand. You can also use thought leadership messaging to seed 'unconsidered needs' of target prospects.

- **Channel partner (indirect) messaging:** The objective with channel partners is to make it easy for them to sell. In order to educate them about the products, produce-specific messaging and direct sales training can also be applied to channel partners. Channel partners are looking for how to add value to grow and differentiate their businesses. Providing product messaging training is not enough. It's important to go beyond product messaging and provide learning modules on topics that will help partners transform or enhance their businesses. This is critical if channel partners sell software as a service (SaaS)-based or technology-based products, since these products are constantly upgraded, refreshed and updated. Depending on partners' strategic objectives, you may need to modify your messaging to match their sales offerings. Or they can take your messaging and modify it to tailor to their own offerings and differentiations. It's not about aligning with your messaging, it's about identifying the right messaging for them so that they can sell better on your behalf. Focus on value-add to your channel partners.

- **Brand messaging:** This is usually led by corporate marketing and focuses on generic and non-product specific messaging. Many companies promote both corporate brand and product brands in parallel. For example: Microsoft is the master brand, while Windows 10, Bing, Xbox are product brands. Messages delivered to customers or end users can be divided into distinct messaging buckets: brand and product.[5]

- **Purchase role specific messaging:** In B2B selling, buyers of products are not necessarily users. Marketing may be building awareness among users, but sales teams need to influence the buying committee, which is likely to comprise IT managers, procurement specialists, VPs of specific departments and others who often are not users of the product. The primary beneficiaries of technical buyer messaging are the sales team. The end-user messaging may be about productivity and ease-of-use, while the messaging for IT managers is likely to be about easy migration and total cost of ownership (TCO) and the messaging for procurement might focus on pricing and terms. Again, they sound different, but they are all grounded under productivity and ease-of-use.

Different journey, consistent messaging

Today's B2B customers conduct more independent research and it takes more time and effort to make a purchase. In addition, their purchase journey may differ from one customer to the next; they're not all listening to the same radio spots or going to the same websites to learn about your company. They're not even being exposed to the same information about your brand from the same sources. Some may have discovered your company on social media, while others learned of your products or services through (virtual) word-of-mouth recommendations. Some may read online reviews before engaging with your marketing team or filling out an online request for more information. Others will visit your website, read your blog, and evaluate your competition before engaging. Therefore, it's important to deliver consistent messaging across channels that your company uses for outbound marketing efforts.

Consistency does not mean rigidity

It's important to differentiate consistency from being rigid and boring. Consistency means adherence to a specific look and feel and tone and manner. You can still exercise a sense of innovation and creativity within that boundary. It comes back to knowing what you are and what makes your customers tick. Delight your customers, yet stay true to your brand essence.

The power of branding and messaging to sales

It's hard to quantify the benefits of brand guides and messaging frameworks in the context of sales revenue. The main effect is to enable other marketing processes and sales tactics and it is only effective when thoroughly adopted by marketing and sales. However, we all have experienced brands we can recognize and that evoke our emotions. Subconsciously, we also value brands as good, bad and neutral through their messaging, visual, copy and their overall look and feel. If marketing is done well and in a consistent way, the target audiences clearly understand what the brands' products can do for them. At that point, it's no longer about the logo or the brand, it's about a clearly received message. Using these documents will lead to shorter sales cycles and drive higher conversions on your websites. But be cognizant that it's not easy to directly tie the results to the brand guide and messaging framework.

Remember

The brand guide is not your brand. Messaging is not your content. They are just resources for you to use. You still need to carefully construct an online and offline presence to build emotional and essential connections with your customers.

You still need to facilitate the buyers' purchase journey. We need to prove our value to our customers. The power of the brand comes from your ability to persuade your customers to buy from you again. The power of messaging helps you differentiate your products and services, attract new customers and retain existing ones. Branding and messaging not only shape marketing communications, but also serve as a baseline for sales engagements. To provide consistent experience through the purchase funnel, branding and messaging should be part of onboarding and sales training development. In addition, these two elements are not just for large corporations. All businesses can use branding and messaging to win a place in their customers' hearts and minds.

What you can do

1 Find your company's brand guide and product messaging framework.

2 Identify how the brand guide and messaging framework can be used for your job and the sales team.

3 Assist your sales team in identifying unconsidered needs and craft messages to address those needs.

Notes

1 Google. Material Design. https://material.io/guidelines

2 Mark Di Somma. 4 ways brands should support sales. *Branding Strategy Insider*, 24 March 2015. www.brandingstrategyinsider.com/2015/03/brands-should-support

3 Erik Peterson, Tim Riesterer, Conrad Smith and Cheryl Geoffrion. *The Three Value Conversations: How to create, elevate, and capture customer value at every stage of the long-lead sale.* McGraw-Hill Education, New York, 2015

4 Myk Pono. Strategic communication: How to develop strategic messaging and positioning. *Medium*, 14 December 2016. https://medium.com

5 Derek Skaletsky. Product vs Marketing Messaging... huh? Knowtify.io. 12 April 2015. http://blog.knowtify.io/product_vs_marketing_messaging

Key sales enablement ingredients

Training, content, and coaching

The purpose of sales enablement is to enhance salespeople's knowledge or change their behaviour.
LEE LEVITT, ORACLE

When I talked to Tamara Schenk, Research Director of CSO Insight, about content and sales training, she immediately posed a question:

> How do you define content and training in the context of sales enablement? Training can mean corporate training, product training, sales technique training and more. And training can come from different departments such as human resources (HR), business units, product groups or marketing, etc. What about content? Do you mean training-specific content or content that the sales team needs throughout their sales processes to engage with their prospects and customers?

She has a point.

Before defining training and content, I decided to review my own definition of effective sales enablement from earlier in this book:

> Deliver a positive customer experience by equipping sales with knowledge, skills, processes, and tools through cross-functional collaboration in order to increase sales velocity, sales retention, and productivity.

I created the definition after my conversation with Tamara. Looking at that definition, I realized that I don't need to define content and training per se. The end result is to arm the sales team with relevant knowledge, essential skills and tools to facilitate conversation at each stage of the sale. Content and training are merely some of the means, in addition to practising pitches, reading, peer-to-peer conversations, coaching and more. In general, when sales teams define training, it means onboarding or continuous training related to knowledge and skills. Knowledge refers to the understanding of products, competitors, industry trends, opportunities, threats and usage of different tools. Skills are more about communications, storytelling, selling techniques, pitches, research and positioning. Content covers not only sales training materials but also assets needed to support sales tactics during sales processes and as part of customer outreach, both on and offline. If salespeople need content to further engage with customers or prospects on social media channels, it would be great to have targeted content readily available for them to curate and share. Bear in mind that content and training are not the only ways for sales to gain knowledge and skillsets. Coaching and facilitation are equally important. Therefore, in this chapter, I'll discuss how to equip sales with knowledge and skills through:

- training:
  - onboarding
  - continuous education
- content:
  - create content to support sales tactics
  - share marketing materials to enable sales
- coaching:
  - prep sales personnel for discovery discussions
  - facilitate conversions through sales stages

Generally, it's not marketing's job to create training and development. However, marketing can easily influence and provide value in this area. I have seen, in some companies, that marketing is responsible for sales' product and tool training; this is especially true when marketing are responsible for product messaging, or of product management reports into marketing. Given that marketers are responsible for external-facing content creation, they can certainly provide input and help in sales-focused content. If marketing sits in sales opportunity review meetings or is part of an account-based selling team, they can provide insights to sales regarding the marketing side of account-based engagements. Marketing can provide value-add to training, content and coaching.

Sales training

The main function of sales enablement is rooted in training and development. Although we are all very quick to relate training to onboarding and regular product and skills training, it's important to take the time to create a sales training plan. Map knowledge and skills with sales processes, sales tactics and sales career tracks. Different knowledge and skills are required for different sales functions and career paths. Inside salespeople need strong verbal communications skills with a high level of product knowledge to either schedule meetings for outside sales or close sales on the phone or via email. They need to quickly assess opportunities, conduct research and present business cases to induce prospects to meet with salespeople or make a purchase. Outside salespeople managing strategic accounts must hone in on one-to-one relationship building and deepen their understanding of accounts' firmographics and technographics. Their skill set focuses on conducting needs analysis, offering recommendations and solutions and preparing proposals. Both inside and outside sales functions need strong communications capability.

You can also slice and dice training plans by product, job function, or even based on sales process and methodology. There are many ways to approach training. Devise a sales training strategy, then apply training development and learning objectives. It gets complicated when you start designing training. You need to take into account the options for learning environments, such as classroom training, multi-media or short spurt micro-learning. We should also consider the devices (laptop vs tablet vs phone vs digital watch or other form factors) that sales personnel will use to consume content. Designing an effective sales training programme really boils down to one question: Will it create long-term change in the behaviour of the salespeople, leading to positive results?[1]

Although it's hard to directly correlate sales training to revenue or hard ROI, training does have a 'rising tide lifts all boats' effect if it's done properly. According to a research report by CSO Insight, *The Business Case for Sales Training*, only 9.6 per cent of the respondents rated their companies' sales training programmes as having 'exceeded expectations'. The results from companies with sales training programmes that 'exceeded expectations' showed a 3 per cent increase in sales reps achieving quota as compared to companies whose sales skills training programmes just met expectations, and an 8 per cent increase in sales reps achieving quota as compared to companies where sales skills training programmes were rated as 'needs improvement'.[2] Long-term change only comes from a repeatable system and structured curriculum.

Onboarding

'Baby, I'm so proud of you; you're going to be paid to enable,' said Amy Pence's mother when Amy told her about her new job offer as the Director of Global Enablement for Alteryx. Before joining Alteryx, Amy was a salesperson, but also dabbled in training, business development, and marketing. She has the most affinity with anything that supports and empowers sales. Even her mother knows that she is an enabler; that says something about Amy's natural skillset.

Before talking to Amy, I had never heard of Alteryx, even though it was ranked number twenty-four on Forbes' 2016 Cloud 100 list.[3] Alteryx's platform makes predictive analytics easy. Their platform allows you to build workflows by prepping, pulling and blending data from various legacy systems. Then, you can use the data on their platform to run regression models or different statistical analyses to forecast or predict the outcomes of various scenarios. The company positions itself as a leading self-service data analytics platform. I didn't fully comprehend the values of their products until I watched their 20-minute product demo. Once I watched it, I could immediately grasp how I would use the platform to aid marketing communications. Since the platform requires explanations and set-up before customers can fully take advantage of the tools, newly hired sales staff need to be properly onboarded, trained and armed with relevant content in order to sell.

Alteryx's management realizes that sales enablement plays a critical role in the sales team's success. Amy was hired for the job in March of 2014, when the company was private. Along with going public in March 2017, there was a push to increase the salesforce. The timing was perfect to leverage Amy's expertise and passion for enabling and empowering her sales team.

When Amy joined Alteryx, management was looking to expand its sales force rapidly to grow its business. Onboarding is critical to getting new hires ready to step onto battlefields. Sales onboarding is called 'sales bootcamp'. The ownership of sales bootcamp was originally under the marketing group. It made sense at that time, since a good chunk of onboarding focused on product training. In 2015, sales bootcamp was reorganized under the sales team, with Amy taking the lead. It shifted its focus from solely product (what to sell) to both product (what to sell) and sales technique (how to sell) training. It made sense to make that transition since sales process and methodology were incorporated into bootcamp training.

When Amy took over sales bootcamp, it was a two-and-a-half-day lecture-driven sales training with lengthy PowerPoint presentations. It was one-way communication. Her approach: let's flip it. Since the bootcamp had to cover product and sales techniques, she extended it from two-and-half days to five days. She also made a conscious effort to make it interactive, with numerous role-playing exercises.

The actual delivery of the five-day bootcamp is managed by facilitators from Amy's team and there are multiple sales representatives as speakers. For each topic, it's usually fifteen to twenty minutes of content followed by question-and-answer and 'whiteboard' discussions, team activities, and role playing. The activities provided opportunities for participants to be hands-on. A great example of a whiteboard discussion is 'the top ten most common objections you will encounter'. An experienced sales rep would talk about the objections (fifteen to twenty minutes of presentation) and ask participants to provide remedies for each objection (whiteboard discussion). In some cases, they will also do a practice-run of real-life situations (role-playing). Lastly, the session leader would give additional suggestions on how to handle the different situations.

When Amy decided to revamp the onboarding, she conducted a quick survey to determine the topics that new hires need to comprehend in the first three month on the job. There were more than twenty topics such as value proposition, market positioning, competitive intel, the Alteryx sales model, and persona empathy. Amy worked with the sales team to prioritize the results. Some are incorporated into the onboarding 'bootcamp', others are delivered as virtual sessions as part of continuous training.

Here is her typical one-day onboarding agenda:

5.1

Agenda

9AM–10AM : STORYTELLING

10AM–10:30AM : DISCOVERY TO DEMO TO DOLLARS

10:30AM–11AM : BREAK

11AM–NOON : SALES STAGES + PLAYBOOK

NOON : LUNCH

1PM–2:30PM : PROJECT WORKSHOP + WHITEBOARD PREP

2:30PM–3PM : BREAK

3PM–4PM : COMPETITIVE CORNER

4PM–5PM : SALESHOOD OVERVIEW

Amy pairs a facilitator with a speaker. The speaker will discuss the topic and go through a short presentation, then the facilitator helps drive exercises, activities and role-playing. One of the key take-aways for new hires after completion of the bootcamp is the whiteboard certification. It forces new hires to internalize product messaging, sales pitches and other information, then, present their own versions of stories to their prospects or customers. During bootcamp, Amy allows participants to create their own versions of whiteboard presentation without the traditional visual aids, such as PowerPoint.

When I talked to Amy, she told me that she redesigned the courses in a couple of weeks and did a quick transition from the two-and-a-half days to five days. She implemented changes based on the sales team's feedback. Sales management made it clear that the bootcamp needs to allocate time to prepare new hires for the whiteboard session. They also wanted a tight agenda and for new salespeople to be kept on their toes and engaged. It was important for new hires to understand the corporate culture and sales organization.

The revised bootcamp has been running once a month since 2016. Overall, it's well received, not only by new hires, but also by sales management. Sales employees feel motivated and ready to get out into the field and help solve their customers' challenges.

Michael King, CMO of Open19 Foundation, shared his sales experience at Limelight Networks. Limelight sell content delivery network services (CDN) to customers such as Netflix, HBO, CBS and others who have rich media to share. They adopted a 'value-selling' methodology. Historically, onboarding to this specific methodology has taken three days. They adopted a train-the-trainer approach and condensed the training into a single day, so it could be included for each new member of the sales team as part of their corporate training. Although they didn't cover all the topics in as much depth, Limelight found that requiring their own marketing and salespeople to deliver the training based on their real-world experience created better cohesion between sales and marketing processes and content, was a better use of their time, and gave their new hires enough of a base to get into the field.

Remember

- Understand sales teams' expectations when designing onboarding.
- Prioritize topics based on the length of training days.
- Balance the mix of product and sales tactic education.
- Minimize lecture-driven approaches and focus on whiteboarding and role-plays.
- Pair a speaker with a facilitator or leverage a train-the-trainer approach based on budget and resource.

Continuous training

Even though the onboarding bootcamp is interactive, inspirational and beneficial, we still need continuous training as a reminder to keep current on new techniques, trends and products. Why? Because we forget information quickly. According to the Ebbinghaus forgetting curve, we forget 42 per cent of what we have learned in twenty minutes. Within thirty-one days, a typical onboarding timeline, we lose 79 per cent of what we learned.[4] To drive behavioural changes and reinforce product messages, continuous training is the yang to onboarding's yin.

Continuous training is like taking your car for maintenance. Your car needs an oil change at regular intervals. Your salespeople are out selling all the time, but they need to come back for regular tune-ups. The marketing landscape may have changed. The competitors may have new product launches and value proposition that need to be communicated. New tools may be available to assist with social selling. Whatever it is, continuous training is like an oil-change and regular maintenance. To be effective continually, it's important to take a break from selling to receive new knowledge, review previous learning, sharpen skills and understand new tools and processes.

John Barrows, a sales manager turned sales trainer, explains the process from his time at Xerox. The company invested heavily in their sales force and trained them well. When he was at Xerox in the late 1990s, any salesperson from Xerox was well regarded and perceived to be well trained. Following in Xerox's footsteps, IBM, Microsoft, Intel, and many other companies also invested heavily in their sales teams. In today's world, Salesforce has taken over the lead in sales training excellence. Salesforce.com has a well-established sales enablement team that focuses on sales development and training. The company also has a four-day bootcamp for their new sales hires. Upon registering for the bootcamp, all salespeople are required to complete pre-work and knowledge checks. To make sure that new salespeople continue to receive the necessary knowledge and skill set, Kimberly Miracle, a Sales Enablement Manager, shared with me that the sales enablement team created a complete six-month structured curriculum of continuous online and offline training that salespeople need to take. The sales enablement team works closely with the new hires and their managers to monitor and track their continuous education journey. Successful sales organizations continuously focus on training after onboarding.

As part of my research, I spoke with Charles (Chuck) Steinhauser. He has been in the technology segment for over three decades and has seen the ebb and flow of this industry. Before Apple, Intel and Microsoft came to the fore, there was a computer company called Digital Equipment Corporation (DEC) where Chuck was a sales manager. In the 1970s, DEC was one of the early pioneers in relatively affordable computers, known as mini-computers, that competed with IBM mainframes. At its peak, DEC was the second largest computer company in the industry. DEC was founded in 1957, evolved and grew at an exciting time in the computer era with numerous software and hardware innovations and technologies popping up like mushroom. Keeping sales up to speed on new product development and the constantly changing marketing landscape was critical at DEC. The marketing department published weekly sales updates and competitive updates to inform the sales team about both DEC's and competitors' moves and product development. Salespeople could decide not to subscribe, but, according to Chuck, these weekly updates were fantastic informal and continuous training.

Although DEC as it was originally formed no longer exists, it created a lasting legacy for today's computing industry, paving the way for current computers, software and microchips. DEC even contributed to the early days of the internet with one of the first search engines, AltaVista. Although there were many causes for its decline, Chuck notes how well DEC treated its employees and how much management was willing to invest in its sales team.

Today Steinhauser is Director of Sales Operations and Enablement for the Broadband, Cables and Satellite division of Amdocs, responsible for implementing similar continuous training for his sales team, but with a modern digital twist. Amdocs offers a comprehensive product portfolio to support the back-end infrastructure and technology for broadband, cable and satellite providers such as Cox Communications, AT&T, Verizon, and other well-known telecom companies. This industry is changing fast. Most Millennials are 'cable cutters', meaning that they don't subscribe to cable for television anymore. They subscribe to content channels via the Internet, such as Netflix, Hulu or Amazon to stream TV shows and films. The business model has switched from the cable model to the content model. Chuck needs to make sure that his sales team stay on top of these trends and the company's complicated portfolio.

He instituted two programmes: 'prime time' and 'on demand.' I love the names because they have synergy with the organization's products! Prime time is a live bi-weekly webinar in which subject matter experts from different products will come to discuss product features, value propositions, speaking points to customers and calls-to-action. On demand is also bi-weekly and focuses on management communications such as pricing, forecasts and deal wins. This is where sales tunes in for continuous training and updates.

For continuous education, Michael King emphasizes the importance of 'training' salespeople to use the available content. When he was at DataDirect Networks, the sales team had regular quarterly business review meetings. Experienced sales managers would share the challenges they encounter when they talk to prospects and existing customers. Then, they would share the solutions to address those issues and the relevant content they use. For example, 'If customers inform you that they do not need centralized storage, here is what you (as the salesperson) should say and what content to use to illustrate your points...' He stresses that knowing which content to use is as important as understanding the customers' challenges. Marketing can help sales put content into context.

Obviously, continuous training can get complicated when you take into account devices (mobile learning) and sales teams' individual learning preferences (self-paced podcasts or webinars or in-person training). You don't have to implement the latest technologies or the most popular channels. The key is to provide quality training with specific channels consistently. As long as the sales team find it beneficial and relevant, they will participate. A key thing to remember is to focus on the quality of your training content.

Remember

- Continuous training is as important as onboarding.
- Continuous training can be delivered with formal and informal approaches.
- Work with the sales team to determine the best formats for continuous training.
- Comprehend the device-based and individual learning preferences.

Training from other departments

Most of the training from other departments tends to be related to topics other than sales. However, sales may require specific training classes, such as code of conduct, insider trading, safety or branding in order to comply with corporate or government regulations. To create a better learning organization, Intel has established Intel U. When I started at Intel, Intel U offered a lot of 'soft skills' courses for employees, with topics like improving presentation skills, active listening, managing a virtual team and more. For different levels of managers, Intel also offered appropriate training courses to improve their people and management skills. Andy Grove, founder of Intel, was fond of saying that employees own their own employability. It's each employee's job to proactively determine the skills and knowledge that they need to pursue their own career path. As a sales enablement person focusing on sales training and development, you can suggest some of these classes as complementary curricula. As a sales professional, some of these outside sales training courses may help you to determine your own future career paths.

Another type of continuous training comes from marketing. It rolls out training for branding, messaging, new product offering, campaign timelines and others to make sure that sales teams are aware of marketing outreach efforts. It's critical to keep sales up to date on the company's marketing efforts, since potential customers may ask the salesperson about a particular promotion or new offering. Digital marketing has made the line between sales and marketing blurry. In some cases, marketing source tools such as social listening and social media for the company's brand ambassadors. These tools can also be used by sales for social selling, account-based sales and prospect outreach. To better enable sales, marketers need to understand the overall sales processes and methodology, help sales connect the dots and identify where best to employ the tools in specific stages of the sales journey.

Remember

- Be aware of other departments' training offerings and incorporate them into the sales curriculum if it's appropriate.
- Work with marketing to incorporate marketing outreach effort updates as part of regular sales communications updates.

Content

Content marketing has been a hot buzz term for the past several years. My first book, *Global Content Marketing*, describes how to scale content across different regions through a collaborative effort between headquarters and local teams. Content is defined as 'anything that conveys meaningful information to humans'.[5] Content can be a video, a blog, a post, an image, a webinar, a tweet, a white paper, an e-book, etc. Buyers and users are acutely aware of their challenges and issues, though they don't necessarily know how to solve them, especially the business solutions involving technologies in which they may not be conversant. Since they do not know what they do not know, they do research. They want to 'learn'. That motivation creates a big opportunity for marketers and sellers to 'educate'.

And the best way to educate or be helpful to your customers is through helpful and relevant content. Content plays a vital role in selling complex technology. People consume content all the time on laptops, tablets and phones, sitting on the couch or searching on-the-go. Therefore, through useful content, marketing not only showcases a company's thought leadership, but also its expertise and knowledge of products or technologies. Based on people's searches,

Google serves up relevant information (aka content) with the aim of answering their questions. Content is also essential for search engine optimization (SEO). To support sales in sales enablement, content comes in the context of internal sales training, internal sales materials for tactics and external marketing materials to share with prospects and customers.

Determining sales training topics

I asked Chuck Steinhauser how he determines his editorial content topics for continuous sales training. He told me that the topics come from marketers, key account managers, and product developers. It can be about products, technologies, competitors or even future trends. He'd confer with all of them on a timely basis to gather their feedback and plan the topics for prime time.

Amy Pence's approach at Alteryx is a little different, but equally effective. She sees her mission as one of improving sales' performance and productivity through training. Amy focuses closely on sales key performance indicators (KPIs). The common KPIs are average sales cycle duration, pipeline growth, deal size, etc. She takes one KPI and works backward to identify the specific activities and knowledge needed to determine the focus of continuous learning. For example: one of the KPIs is 'pipeline multiplier'. She would review the qualification activities to understand the possible causes of many disqualified leads. Were the messaging and talking points strong during the discovery conversation? Was the salesperson properly trained and informed? Was the contact and related data of a lead inaccurate? She then uses this data to identify training topics to address those causes. It's a lot of work and educated guesses, but I think it's very smart to tie training course offerings to KPIs.

Understand sales needs to create sales-focused content

A marketing person supporting sales content is different from a marketing person creating marketing content. Marketing content tends to be broad and tailored to awareness-focused or top-of-the-funnel communications. The reach and frequency are key at the top of the funnel. Most of the time, marketing's job is completed after capturing marketing qualified leads and passing them to inside sales or a sales development representative (SDR). Although sales content such as product briefs, case studies and pricing/feature comparison guides are standard as buyers move through the sales stages, content required for various conversations and meetings throughout the stages is customized and personalized.

Supporting sales by providing content as a marketing person can be tricky. You need to apply judgement as to when to use standard content or customized content to support varied tactics. To do that well, you need to *think* and *act* like a salesperson. Diane Walker, a former Sales Enablement Manager for SAP and McAfee, took the sales onboarding class, attended all subsequent sales training classes and took all the online modules. She made an effort to 'walk a mile' in the sales team's shoes. Once she was able to walk the walk and talk the talk, she could proactively help her sales teams with presentations, positioning and pulling information from various sources.

Share marketing materials to enable sales

Marketing creates a lot of content for multiple communications purposes. Depending on sales stages or conversations with customers, product-specific content tends to be frequently requested by the sales team. Content that marketing creates that would also work for sales communications includes:

5.2

PRODUCT VIDEOS   PRODUCT PAGES ON WEB   SOLUTION BRIEFS   CUSTOMER STORIES   CASE STUDIES

ROI REPORTS   WHITE PAPERS/ TRENDS   COMPETITOR COMPARISONS   TOPIC-SPECIFIC WEB CONTENT

These types of content come in handy and should be part of the sales playbook or part of the sales portal, especially as a follow-up to a productive conversation or meeting. According to research, there is a picture superiority effect that indicates people will remember only 10 per cent of what you say within two days of your meeting. That means that in a very short period of time they will have forgotten the vast majority of what you were trying to convey.[6] Therefore, after conversations and meetings, it's important to share content to validate, reinforce or remind customers of your key points. Some of this content can also be used by salespeople for their own mini-email outreach campaigns. Even if sales reps are either waiting to hear back from prospects or trying to re-engage with existing customers, using some of these content pieces is a non-intrusive tactic to keep those relationships warm. Content, in both cases, keeps the brand on the top-of-the-mind of your customers and prospects.

As a marketer supporting sales, it's essential to have an overview of the most current content available so you can pull the best recommendations from your content trove during opportunity reviews, sales pipeline update meetings, or informal chats with your salespeople.

Remember

- Understand sales' content needs by completing onboarding, continuous training and actively participating in key sales customer discussions.
- Discover new sales training topics through interviews with relevant stakeholders or KPI analysis.
- Incorporate relevant content into the sales playbook or the sales portal so that sales teams have easy access.

Coaching

I had a conversation with Lee Levitt, Manager of Sales Excellence for Oracle, who has been working in sales for over twenty years. One of the primary roles in his job is coaching and facilitation. He believes that training has its place, but sometimes, what sales need is to have a person to talk to about the challenges they encounter.

It's about talking things through to crystalize their thinking processes and determine the actionable next steps to move a sale forward. It's a coaching/therapy/brainstorming session. That's what Levitt does.

Prepare sales personnel for discovery discussions

Coaching and facilitation can play a key role in the discovery stage of a targeted account. An example that Levitt uses is when the account team identified the key decision maker of a major purchase. They were trying to plan the first meeting with the decision maker, but they were struggling with a key message point to anchor the initial conversation. Based on the team's research, they found out that this person had been with the company for twelve years. He was a private pilot and avid scuba diver. What can we assume about his personality? What was his view of the world: risk-taking or risk-averse? What can we say that will appeal to his specific view of the world? On the surface, this person – a pilot and scuba diver – is seemingly a risk-taker. But pilots and scuba divers make sure they have solid back-ups to minimize risk. He probably thinks everything through before he flies or dives. Therefore, the assumption was made that this person wasn't a 'revenue guy' (more aggressive than measured) – he is a 'risk manager'. Based on that insight, the sales team created a plan for the first conversation with the decision maker that focused on minimizing his risk. The sales team's research and insight proved worthwhile and led to successfully building a good rapport at their first meeting. Part of sales enablement's function is to arm the sales team with the ability to discover what makes a prospect tick and tie it to the sales cycle.

Improve conversions during sales stages

One key objective of sales coaching is to help sales reps break through impasses, which was another example from my conversation with Levitt. One of the sales teams he supported sold datacentres to IT departments. One prospect had been telling the sales manager that his datacentre capacity was at capacity. Obviously, he needed to purchase additional capacity; however, the sales team had not been able to close the purchase with the IT manager, even though the sales manager knew that the IT manager had the budget.

Lee met with the sales manager and started asking the sales manager a list of questions (like a therapist in a way), such as how long has the datacentre been at capacity? Was it maxed out for six months or two years? How did he get by for this long? Can he get by for another two years and why? What were the major business initiatives that may impact the usage of the datacentre in the next three to six months? Most importantly, what was it going to cost the IT manager if he didn't act now based on his requirement? Can we get the conversation to the point that a datacentre addition is an urgent and compelling event? Lee defines a compelling event as a trigger point that the IT manager needs to act on to avoid future and probable disaster. In other words, if something is not done now, there will be a serious negative impact to the business. Levitt's job was to continue to ask questions to help the sales manager identify a specific compelling event that could propel the conversation with the IT manager.

Levitt's approach is very similar to Erik Peterson's approach. In his book *The Three Value Conversations*, he shared the concept 'make the status quo unsafe'. Peterson asserts that buyers are dissatisfied with the status quo, but it's safe. Buyers know there are issues, but they can still get by day to day. So, why rock the boat? Buyers will only react if the status quo becomes unsafe. 'Convincingly showing them how they will lose out by not doing something gives them a sense of urgency – especially when you are able to show them the problem is bigger and badder than they realize'. Using a compelling event to drive a decision is also one of the tactics in the NEAT selling methodology – need, economic impact, access to authority, timeline.

Then I asked Levitt a question: how does he scale coaching and facilitation? Coaching and facilitation are great, but it works best in one-on-one settings. He mentioned that he could scale by doing an opportunity review call with a group of sales managers. Again, it's about helping sales reps to find their own compelling event trigger point to move their prospects to the next stage. During one particular call, a sales woman mentioned that her inside champion has a management by objective (MBO) to get the system running by January. Bingo! That's the compelling event! Her prospect has a specific action that needs to be done by January. The sales rep can easily use that as an anchor! Her answer forced other sales team members to think through what their compelling events might be. Having an opportunity review with several sales managers is a way to scale coaching.

From Levitt's perspective, coaching through conversations is experiential learning. It's a different style of learning. Through conversations, he guides sales managers to think differently when they encounter similar challenges in the future. It's about changing their thinking and behaviour over time. The ability to address a problem in a different way comes from coaching and facilitation, not lecture-driven training. It's about helping sales teams to think through their own sales tactics and help them get unstuck.

Levitt acknowledges that coaching is not something that can be scaled massively. However, everything starts with baby steps. His conversations with sales team members help them understand how to work through their roadblocks and, after working through several issues this way, they begin to understand how to do it on their own. In this way he helped to change their behaviours. Salespeople know how to sell, but from time to time they need someone to help them tweak their techniques. Just as in the world of sports where the world's top tennis players still have coaches – they know how to play tennis well, but they sometimes need a fresh viewpoint to derive new strategies to continue improving their results.

Remember

- Although not every sales organization has 'sales coaches', experienced sales manager can act as a sales mentor or coach to help fellow sales colleagues get 'unstuck' from a sales impasse.

- As a salesperson who evaluates opportunity, it's important to proactively seek guidance and support to get past potential barriers.

- If necessary, escalate and seek management support.

Integrate training, content, and coaching

Emma Hitzke is a Senior Marketing Manager for Intel's IoT division. Her biggest challenges were enabling sales in an organization. 'Silos! Silos are the underlying obstacle to getting sales, marketing and other functions working together efficiently.' So true! Silos prevent us from changing organizational structures, reconciling diverse sales and marketing goals, or even eliminating office politics or poor corporate culture. One way to break down silos is to align marketing and sales from the outset in order to tackle potential key accounts.

Account-based selling has been around for a long time. Marketing can support account-based selling by running a series of campaigns targeted at specific accounts. Sales and marketing work side by side to deliver timely content and engagement to the right people in the right context.

A popular concept is account-based marketing (ABM), a strategic approach that combines targeted, insight-led marketing with sales to increase mindshare, strengthen relationships and drive growth in specific new and existing accounts. The IT Services Marketing Association has identified three types of ABM:

- **strategic ABM:** one-on-one
- **ABM lite:** one-to-few
- **programmatic ABM:** one-to-many

In any of these types of ABM efforts, the team will need a tool to orchestrate and collaborate with all relevant internal and external players. This tool also needs to pull data from different sources and portals to help you make decisions on targeted accounts. The challenge is what data to pull and how you leverage the data to determine the key accounts.

Iris Chan, CMO of Fusion Grove, recommends that teams working together on ABM need to do their homework to understand their target accounts before initiating customized marketing efforts. She emphasizes that a customer's propensity to buy hinges on three attributes – fit, intent and engagement.

Fit: The set of environmental factors and attributes of a company that make it likely to need your offering

They are generally identified by two types of data – firmographics and technographics. As described earlier, firmographic data refers to attributes about the company, for example the number of employees, annual revenue, industry vertical and number of branch offices. If your offering is designed for small/medium-sized businesses, you would not want to target companies with 80,000 employees! If your solution has strong use cases in healthcare, then you would want to apply the industry filter to narrow down your efforts to organizations in that vertical. Technographics refers to the potential accounts' technology and organizational environment. These accounts would want to ensure your offerings integrate and fit into their existing infrastructures and applications. Technographics profiles the technologies and related attributes installed or used by organizations, in short, their technology stack.

Intent: Behavioural indicators showing an intention to buy

Basic examples of intent could be questions or comments about a subject related to your offering on social media, announcements of expansion in business operations in new markets or a project starting or underway, a request for proposal (RFP) or the creation of new positions or teams.

Engagement: Activity from all the people who are interacting with your company at the account level

For example, three individuals from the same company spending time on your product web pages is a clear sign they are learning about your solutions.

These levers of analysis will help you decide on the best way to go about creating account-based marketing and selling efforts. Iris, specifically, stresses the importance of fully understanding a company's technology stack:

5.3

ENABLE SALES TEAM
DEMONSTRATE RELEVANCE IN CONTEXT
OF CURRENT TECHNOLOGY INVESTMENTS

SAVE TIME
AND EFFORT ENABLING SALES TEAM
TO FOCUS ON HIGH-VALUE ACCOUNTS

LEVERAGE INSIGHTS
AND INTERSECT WITH YOUR
OWN CUSTOMER DATABASE

- **Enable** the sales team to demonstrate greater levels of business relevance when talking to customers and position their solution in the context of the account's current technology investments. You can hyper-personalize messaging in your campaign or engagement.

- **Save** sales team time and effort by enabling them to focus on those high-propensity, high-value accounts that are most likely to convert. Combined with firmographic detail, you can prioritize and target these high-value accounts with greater predisposition to buy your solutions, which means you get better conversion rates for your campaigns and pipeline acceleration.

- **Leverage** these augmented insights and intersect with your own customer base data to identify different kinds of opportunities, for instance cross-sell, upsell, competitive and complementary solution sales, expansion, renewal/refresh, etc.

Because of the strong focus on specific accounts, the success of ABM is underpinned by strong alignment between sales and marketing, which creates an opportunity for collaboration with sales enablement.

Remember

- Account-based marketing is one of the approaches to break down silos among sales enablement, sales operations, marketing and sales.
- Make an effort to understand customers' needs to through three attributes: fit, intent and engagement.
- It's critical to understand both firmographics and technographics.
- Customize messaging and marketing campaigns at an account-level.

Iris's recommendation is to create a set of step-by-step guides, with details on how the seller should engage the customer, conversation starters, sales tools and calculators, objection handling and other techniques that are tailored for the specific ABM plan or campaigns. One of the pitfalls to avoid in ABM is deploying campaigns that are rich in customer-facing content and messaging but missing or lacking in sales enablement content. In fact, ABM leaders need to work very closely with their sales enablement teams during the planning of ABM programmes to integrate enablement content and resources throughout the process.

Account-based efforts serve as a forcing function to allow sales and marketing to work together. Training, content and coaching are utilized throughout conversations and collaboration among the team members. The greatest impact of training, content and coaching truly comes from the team working together to ensure everyone applies their knowledge and skills with proper tools and processes.

The path to sales enablement mastery is through teamwork and the journey never ends.

What you can do

1   As a marketer supporting sales, attend sales onboarding classes and training modules.

2   Identify marketing content that can be helpful for the sales journey.

3   Start with a small project or targeted account (ABM) to break down the silos between sales and marketing.

Notes

1   David Mattson. Four steps to designing an effective sales training program.www.trainingindustry.com/magazine/issue/four-steps-to-designing-an-effective-sales-training-program

2   Norman Behar. Study reveals the importance of sales training. www.salesreadinessgroup.com/blog/study-reveals-the-importance-of-sales-training

3   Finsmes. Forbes release first list of top 100 cloud companies + 20 rising
    stars. www.finsmes.com/2016/09/forbes-releases-first-list-of-top-100-
    cloud-companies.html

4   Aaron Ross. You need a sales system – not just sales training.
    www.salesforce.com/blog/2016/11/sales-system-sales-training.html

5   Erin Kissane. *The Elements of Content Strategy*, A Book Apart, USA,
    2010

6   ErikPeterson, Tim Riesterer, Conrad Smith and Cheryl Geoffrion.
    *The Three Value Conversations: How to create, elevate and capture
    customer value at every stage of the long-lead sale*, McGraw-Hill
    Education, New York, 2015

All marketing leads to sales

06

I do believe the modern sales leader has to be a marketer.
MATT GORNIAK, SVP OF SALESFORCE.COM

One of my favourite business quotes comes from Peter Drucker, the great thinker of modern management: 'Because the purpose of business is to create a customer, the business enterprise has two – and only two – basic functions: marketing and innovation. Marketing and innovation produce results; all the rest are costs.'[1] His observation is spot-on. Marketing's job is to create and retain customers to enable sales. Therefore, marketing programmes must have an element designed to successfully drive sales conversions.

Attending the US Open Tennis Championships has been on our family's to-do list for over ten years. My husband went to the US Open every year when he was growing up in New York. He's always wanted to take us to experience one of the Grand Slam events. We finally went to the US Open in 2015.

The USTA Tennis Center in Flushing Meadows is a beautiful 46-acre venue with 33 courts including three stadiums. We bought tickets for the first and second days. It was chaotic in the morning on the opening day and took 30 minutes just to get through the security gate. As a first-timer, I was amazed at how well attended this event was. Parents and grandparents take their children and spend the entire day at the venue. People of all ages come from all over the world. Except for Arthur Ashe Stadium (the centre court), you can move around from court to court and watch your favourite tennis players compete and practise.

As a marketer, I had my marketing lenses on when I walked around the venue. Like any popular sporting event, the venue was set up with booths, experience zones, and VIP lounges that were sponsored by different brands. American Express offered an AMEX Fan Center. Everyone could walk in to cool down (it was hot!) on the first floor of its Fan Center. It also provided a members-only lounge on the second floor with portable battery cases for charging phones. That was a nice touch.

Marketing is no longer just marketing

What does this Fan Center have to do with sales enablement? Not so much on the surface. The lounges are viewed as 'event sponsorship' or outbound marketing. Under the surface these lounges are really 'product benefits' for AMEX credit card holders. If customers have AMEX cards, they can enjoy the privilege of staying in the lounge. In a way, this event sponsorship is a sales enablement effort of offering existing members a benefit and touting the VIP benefit to prospects. It serves well for the top of the funnel (awareness-driven) and also the bottom of the funnel (customer-services). The sales team can also use it as a unique talking point and differentiator to sell more cards or to encourage their existing customers to upgrade their cards (upsell). So, this multi-million dollar event sponsorship is a marketing programme with sales enablement flair! It hits four birds with one stone by working in several ways:

1 Marketing outreach and brand awareness.
2 Product highlights and benefits.
3 Unique and targeted sales messaging.
4 Upsell and cross-sell opportunities.

Most salespeople care about marketing activities that bring home the bacon, aka high-quality marketing qualified leads (MQLs). Although salespeople may not focus on where the lead comes from, they certainly want to know about the lead's journey. For example: the lead attended a trade show, stopped by the booth, attended a webinar, and downloaded three pieces of content. They may not care how hard marketing worked to make that happen, but sales reps working hard to convert an MQL to a sales qualified lead (SQL) would want to know which trade show, what webinar and which content pieces the lead saw, so that they can gain valuable insights and start a personalized conversation to convert this MQL into an SQL.

With the rise of digital communications, prospects and existing customers are reading, browsing, conversing, and researching *all the time*. Sales reps may need to do additional research on their own to get a sense of what else a lead did beyond the activities tracked on the company's website. The additional research can include a Google search on the lead, browsing the person's LinkedIn and other social media profiles, checking his or her comments, shares and followers. Assuming the conversation with a prospect goes well, your sales teams may need to follow up with a customized case study via email or even direct the lead to the company's e-commerce site to view alternate options or products. In a way, sales teams are marketers using different marketing tactics to follow up with prospects. The boundary between sales and marketing continues to blur.

In addition, marketing programmes are not so simple and discrete anymore. They can morph into a customer service platform, a product benefit, a sales communications tool and more, like the USTA American Express Fan Center. Other marketing programmes such as co-marketing, if used effectively, can be a bargaining chip for the sales teams during contract negotiations. As a salesperson, you need to have a sense of different marketing programmes within your company. Some of the marketing programmes can be perks for new prospects, such as receiving free points or rewards by joining loyalty or partner programmes. As a sales rep, you don't need to know how the programmes are run, but you need to understand enough about them to know whether they can further your conversations with prospects or help seal a deal. At the same time, it's equally critical for marketers supporting sales to have a holistic view of a company's marketing programmes. With that understanding, you can better help sales connect the dots during opportunity reviews or sales discussions.

In this chapter, I'd like to explore some marketing programmes. They are not part of the sales enablement programme per se, but, if they are used creatively, they can be valuable tools to help sales deliver a better customer experience and increase the velocity of the buyer's journey.

5.1

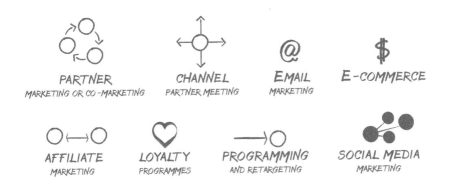

| PARTNER | CHANNEL | EMAIL | E-COMMERCE |
| MARKETING OR CO-MARKETING | PARTNER MEETING | MARKETING | |

| AFFILIATE | LOYALTY | PROGRAMMING | SOCIAL MEDIA |
| MARKETING | PROGRAMMES | AND RETARGETING | MARKETING |

Partner marketing or co-marketing

Partner marketing is when two or more brands collaborate on promotional efforts. Partner marketing comes in different forms. Walmart, the biggest grocery franchise in the US, partnered with Coke to create the 'Stock up on joy' commercial in 2011.[2] It encouraged Walmart shoppers to purchase Coke during the holidays. Its dual purpose was to increase foot traffic in Walmart and increase Coke sales. This is an example of classic partner marketing collaboration between two brands to increase sales and brand awareness. It's a win–win.

In the tech industry, partner marketing is a key channel for driving demand for new technologies. To build the PC ecosystem and create PC demand, Intel established co-marketing efforts with Dell, HP, Asus, Microsoft, and more. Intel did not just manufacture a microprocessor. In the early days, Intel sales and marketing worked tirelessly with manufactures to help them design motherboards for desktops and laptops to establish a strong PC ecosystem. With original equipment manufacturers (OEMs) and original design manufacturers (ODMs), the company not only developed co-marketing campaigns, but also negotiated to have Intel logo stickers placed on desktops and laptops. But that was not enough for consumers to know what Intel offered. Intel cleverly positioned the microprocessor as the brain of the computer. They launched the massive Intel Inside marketing campaigns in the early 1990s[3] by encouraging consumers to look for the Intel Inside label when purchasing their personal computers. It was a brilliant move, with a strong alignment between sales and marketing.

6.2

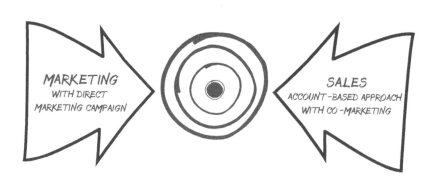

- On the marketing front: it delivered a clear and unique product positioning with massive direct marketing campaigns.

- On the sales side: it provided a strategic account-based approach coupled with co-marketing elements to incentivize vendors to promote PCs.

In a way, Intel doubled its air-cover to include both direct and indirect marketing (co-marketing) efforts. Through consistent marketing outreach, Intel was able to build its awareness steadily. In addition to relentless innovation on the technology front, I firmly believe the enormous PC growth in the 1980s and 1990s can be partially attributed to various partnerships amongst component suppliers, software companies and OEMs and ODMs. They worked together to foster a brand new industry and make it thrive.

Partner marketing can also work well for smaller companies. Jobi George, VP of Business Development and International Operations at StreamSets, shared his partner marketing story with me. Since corporate data typically comes from different systems, StreamSets help companies manage and organize dataflow in pipelines. They call themselves air traffic control for data. StreamSets does not have a big marketing budget. To make their marketing dollars go further, they choose partners who complement their solutions. 'Together is better' helps them present a strong solution for their joint target customers. Cloudera, a platform for machine learning and analytics optimized for the cloud, doesn't offer the dataflow performance management that StreamSets do. If they work together, they create a better end-to-end solution for their target customers. So, they partnered to create joint messaging. StreamSets positions itself as an ideal solution for data input into the Cloudera infrastructure. They attend industry conferences together. They develop target lists to invite each other's customers to attend special events. They also do webinars incorporating both platforms and create joint white papers and other content. Jobi said it clearly: 'The purpose of partner marketing is to make one plus one equal more than two. At the end of the day, it's about creating more customers for both companies.'

The impact of partner marketing on sales enablement

Co-marketing or partner marketing is usually a strategic initiative directed by top management based on senior sales executives' recommendations. It's about how two companies collaborate to deliver more value for themselves and their customers. In big enterprises, both parties may contribute a certain amount of marketing budget as marketing development funds (MDF) for joint marketing campaigns. Marketing managers from both companies need to work together on joint messaging, creative development and a media plan. Smaller companies leverage each other's existing resources and sales efforts. When resource and budgets are constrained, you need to get creative and think outside the box. It may sound easy, but it's hard work, requiring a great deal of back-and-forth collaboration between the two companies. A strategic partnership can take a long time to set up and finalize but, when it's implemented correctly, it generates new demand for both companies. Another objective that you accomplish through co-marketing is to create joint solutions, especially for smaller companies that are often about offering 'best in breed' integration using products from multiple companies. The resulting solution solves a customer problem that none of the component parts could accomplish by themselves. By co-marketing a complete solution and solving the customers' problems, everyone wins.

Remember

- Identify potential co-marketing partners based on strategic and product alignment.
- Create joint solutions to address your customers' needs.
- Define co-marketing objectives, strategy, marketing elements and success metrics.
- Assign one marketing manager to work on the execution of marketing elements. Note: don't underestimate the workload required to do co-marketing well.
- Evaluate co-marketing campaign results against success metrics.

Channel partner marketing

A channel partner is an individual or business that sells products or services on behalf of technology or service providers, manufacturers and hardware or software vendors. While they are part of the sales force, they are not involved with direct sales and instead form part of the indirect sales team for companies. Examples of channel partners are distributors, value-added resellers, system integrators, managed service providers and even retailers. Some may consider channel partner marketing to be another form of partner marketing. To some extent, it is. However, partner marketing tends to be strategic and both partners are on an equal footing. Marketing and sales enablement are a two-way relationship. Channel partners rely heavily on technology or service providers to extend marketing and sales support, provide MDF, relevant product content and, in some cases, share leads. The support is more one-way from technology providers to channel partners.

Traditionally, direct sales and indirect sales don't talk to each other frequently. Occasionally, they will run into each other chasing the same accounts. So, who should have the account? There is no right or wrong answer to this. The best approach is to address issues up-front to minimize channel conflict. Jonathan Crowe, Openview's Senior Content

Manager, suggested addressing the key issues of pricing, compensation, territory and process:[4]

- **Pricing:** Provide channel partner discounts and fixed price points for direct sales to avoid price undercutting.

- **Compensation:** Reward the internal sales team even if the sale goes indirect.

- **Territory:** Segment products by industry verticals or geographical territories, if it's appropriate.

- **Lead registration system:** Channel partners can register a specific number of high-quality leads into a system that direct sales can view. If a lead expires at a certain time, they can re-register it if they are still actively working with it. It allows one lead per rep. Lead and opportunity registration systems serve a similar purpose.

There are other ways to minimize channel conflicts and maintain relationships. David Skok, a board member of Hubspot, observes: 'Why would you intentionally reduce your initial profit by handing the deal off to a partner? Simple. Because it's an investment in creating a channel relationship that will deliver exponentially more value in the long run.'

In general, channel partner engagements don't have a direct relationship with a company's direct sales. Cisco, somehow, built synergy between direct sales and channel partners. Jeff McKittrick, Senior Director, Digital Sales Platforms at Cisco, is part of Cisco's Global Sales Strategy and Operations Leadership team. This team looks at sales success in a holistic way. In collaborating with marketing, product engineering, channel partners, customer success, finance, sales training and IT, this team enables sales growth, productivity and customer/partner satisfaction. He and his team created a digital sales platform, SalesConnect, to support the direct sales team in March 2014. As sales teams from channel partners discovered that the content on SalesConnect was useful to them, the user base grew to over 150,000 Cisco channel partner users. The site has since expanded its content to include online demos and onsite product testing.

The impact of channel marketing on sales enablement

When the term 'sales enablement' is discussed, people tend to focus on support to the direct sales team. Bob Meindl, Director of Content Marketing at Cisco, pointed out that sales enablement on the direct side should also apply to the indirect side. He said: 'Whatever we do to train direct sales to sell the products, you have to do the same for the partners.' It's important to also provide similar support to the indirect sales team. Sales training, sales collateral or marketing materials used by a company's direct sales force can also be used to support the sales force of its channel partners.

In the supplier–reseller relationships, conflict may arise due to both parties wanting to maximize sales. This can be resolved in open discussions between the direct and indirect sales team. For direct sales, channel partners may come to the rescue when there is a deal that may require third party support. In this situation, direct sales may involve a channel partner as part of the deal to ensure customer success. With some situations, direct sales can also do matchmaking and refer leads to channel partners. It's not about direct sales vs indirect sales. It's about motivating both sales forces and creating a mutually beneficial relationship that grows both businesses.

Remember

- If you manage an indirect sales force, it's critical to review your direct sales training, tools and content. Pick and choose what may apply to the indirect sales team.
- Create a sales portal to share content between the direct and indirect sales forces.
- Set up a process for how leads are managed or distributed to channel partners and how the direct force will be compensated.

Email marketing

I love a marketing-programme-turned-sales-differentiator example from Tom Martin, author of *The Invisible Sale*.[5] Several years ago,

Martin was leading an agency team that was working with the sales team of a hotel property to win a deal with an association to host its annual conference. To help this hotel property differentiate itself without getting into a bidding war with other hotel properties, the agency created a turn-key email 'register for the conference' programme. The hotel's sales team offered to execute the email programme for the association at no additional cost if it booked its conference at hotel properties. Although the hotel property didn't get the business because of other factors, it certainly was a great example of using email marketing as a sales value proposition.

Even if email is not used as a sales tool, it is certainly the most common tool used by both sales and marketing. Email is 'not the shiny new thing, but more the steady thing that actually works,' says Neeru Paharia, Assistant Professor of Marketing at Georgetown's McDonough School of Business.[6] Mailchimp, an email marketing service provider, was selected as the company of the year by *Inc. Magazine* in 2017. Forrester estimated US businesses spent $2.8 billion on email marketing in 2017. In the age of Facebook paid ads, Google's paid search and Snapchat's filters, email marketing is still a big and necessary player. All of us complain about how many spam emails we receive, but email is still considered an effective direct marketing channel and the core element of marketing automation and CRM. As part of sales tactics to qualify a lead, sales development reps usually have a specific cadence that they follow, such as seven attempts to reach leads over fifteen days with three calls, three emails and a LinkedIn message. Email is certainly a common channel for account-based marketing to share content and engage with target individuals. Sales and marketing are using email marketing to communicate, nurture, upsell/cross-sell and more.

Martin also shared an example of running campaigns to find hot and warm leads in a company's existing email database. Martin has a unique point of view about email marketing: using email to glean new information from existing prospects. According to him, the ROI of email marketing is not just about revenue, but also gathering intelligence. He stressed that, for certain email marketing efforts, you should not care if prospects or customers buy or make it all the way to lead gen forms. The purpose of these email marketing campaigns is to drive traffic to your sites so that prospects can start clicking and consuming information – this is an important element of the buyer's journey, especially when sales cycles are long and require multiple touchpoints. Every click amounts to a behavioural cue or signal that you can use to segment potential customers behaviourally into a specific profile. 'Profiling' is essential in customizing and personalizing email to your audiences.

Martin suggested marketers develop a behaviour email logic (BEL) diagram. Some may call it a customer journey map or a drip campaign. To create a BEL, you first need to define the core message content of each email you plan to send. The design or selection of core messages depends on your objective or the intelligence that you want to gather. If you want to find warm leads, your content needs to entice prospects who are currently evaluating different solutions or interested in exploring different options and you must create a compelling buying event. Hypothesize what prospects' behavioural patterns are telling you when they click content and move through the BEL. The most time-consuming piece is selecting or creating content and building the content logic sequence of your email marketing.

6.3

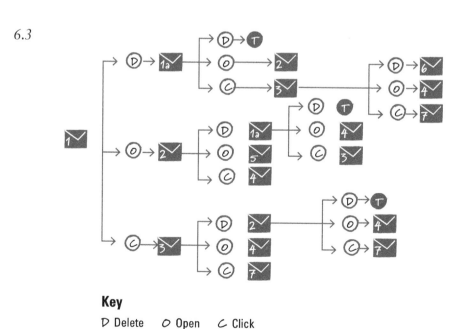

Key

D Delete   O Open   C Click

Here is a sample of a behavioural email diagram based on 'Deleted', 'Opened' and 'Clicked a link in' the email. Martin suggested setting up rules: if prospects open two emails in a row without a click, they receive a specific third message. If they click on two emails in a row, they receive a different message. And so forth through all the possible delete/open/click patterns. The goal of the BEL is simple: through the predefined sequence with carefully crafted content, it's possible to understand what delete/open/click behaviours communicate and segment prospects accordingly. Although all these can be done using sophisticated marketing automaton platforms such as Marketo, Eloqua, Pardot and others, it's important to think through the construction and approach to the BEL, as stated by Martin. The tools are here to help us, but we still need to source appropriate content, internalize the data, review the platform's recommendations and draw our own conclusions.

The impact of mail marketing on sales enablement

Martin uses the BEL diagram to run email campaigns for his clients. The campaigns take about six weeks because you need to give prospects time to act on the emails. He discovered that prospects either act on an email almost immediately or save it for later reading. Based on his experience, they usually come back to the email within three to five days. Thus, he suggests sending each wave seven to ten days apart, to give prospects ample time to respond. Once the campaign has run through the existing database of contacts, the data can be analysed. Martin can usually identify warm leads who had open emails, clicked on links in emails and read a few items on the websites. In addition to the warm leads, there are also a small percentage of hot leads. Martin's recommendations resonate with me based on my own email efforts. However, it's important to run your own email campaigns and customize reach and frequency from your own results.

Behaviour-based analysis can help highlight that contacts not only opened emails, but also clicked on more than one email and/or read multiple items on the websites. In some cases, these prospects visited a lead gen form page on the website. The cold prospects (that did not unsubscribe from your email waves) may indicate a willingness to receive additional email. However, this may not be true if the email has landed in the contact's spam folder. If prospects consistently receive emails and have never opened it, you may consider sending a 'Dear John' final attempt email such as 'Are you still interested in receiving emails from us? If so, then click here' to an auto unsubscribe process. One side note: if you also identify that multiple contacts from the same company never seem to open emails, that could be an indicator that your marketing emails are getting blocked globally at the server level. If you have no way of verbally finding out if a contact has seen your email, it may be difficult to ascertain if emails are even getting through.

You can use the same diagram to qualify leads from trade shows, advertising and general networking. The biggest hurdle is the time it takes to create, launch and then optimize the programme.

Remember

- Email marketing still has its place in the overall marketing outreach.
- Don't send email for the sake of just doing email marketing. Be strategic and select content with well-written copywriting to help identify warm leads or align with email communications objectives.
- Email marketing can be a sophisticated tool to induce specific behaviour with carefully crafted copywriting and content through a series of well-designed and coherent email journeys.
- Email campaign content should be part of the editorial planning discussion.

E-commerce

I am not much of a shopper, and I only shop when I need something. I had never experienced Black Friday shopping until 2013 (and then it was only due to a request from my teenage son). During the 2017 holiday season, when several chairs of our dining table set started falling apart, I went shopping at Macy's, JC Penny, and Dania Furniture stores. I found a style that I liked, and it happened to be on sale. The salesperson, Odette, told me that I could get a 20 per cent New Year sales discount and an additional 15 per cent if I paid using a JC Penny credit card. Sounded good! When it was time to pay, she, as a salesperson, actually went through the whole process via the JC Penny's e-commerce website. She said that it's faster than using the point of sale system. Here she is: a salesperson using the e-commerce workflow to complete the in-store sales transaction. When I asked her if the e-commerce site has any impact on her commissions, she said that e-commerce is her virtual showroom. Many of her customers would browse the JC Penny e-commerce site to view the products and specs, then they come to the store, ask her questions about their choices and complete transactions in person. She told me that some people prefer going through the whole buying process online, while some prefer doing research online and completing transactions in person. It's very much a personal preference.

I've heard that e-commerce is eating sales' commission. But this doesn't need to be the case if sales' compensation is structured properly. E-commerce should be treated as another channel for the sales teams, not a direct competitor. 'Successful B2B e-commerce leaders actually pay sellers a higher rate for business done online in their territories,' says the Blue Sky Technology Partner blog. Not only does this create an environment where reps and the online store empower each other, but sellers can achieve higher-revenue goals since they are not spending time taking orders.'[7]

The impact of e-commerce on sales enablement

Another big advantage of e-commerce is the ability to address channel partners' need to access product information and specifications. 'Providing dealers with their own branded web stores, pre-loaded with product information and content, allows you to scale very powerful e-commerce tools to your resellers who might not have the same resources to invest in their online channel. It's little use trying to improve your customer experience if you don't do the same for the reseller experience' (from the same blog).

E-commerce is also a convenient way for customers to order replacement parts, as opposed to having sales take the order. When customers order replacement parts on the Caterpillar e-commerce site, Caterpillar is able to track and assign the name of the dealer who manages that customer. Caterpillar will make sure that the dealer receives the proper commission, even though the order does not come from the dealer directly.

E-commerce also works well for SaaS with business models of 'freemium' (whereby a product or service is provided free of charge, but money is charged for additional features, services, or virtual goods) or self-subscribed transactions. It's not about eliminating the sales force. Sales teams should see it as an opportunity to increase sales and build prospects for future upgrades or cross-selling and upselling. This creates opportunities for buyers who are ready to buy, but is also a win–win in that it makes it simple for the customer to buy without taking up sales team resources.

The success of e-commerce projects, especially in B2B, requires input from the sales team. To set up the buying workflow, sales reps who talk to customers all the time can tell the project team how the customers buy. In addition, depending on your organizational culture, you may need the sales team's approval or risk jeopardizing your e-commerce development with lacklustre effort or even active attempts to derail your projects. It's important to have the sales team's buy-in.

If your products are complex and require different custom configurations and/or steps to set up, then you are likely to need a multi-stage process, which takes longer. Having sellers gather requirements and send emails back and forth, for example, opens the door to mistakes, blind spots, and dissatisfaction. Online tools can fix this with much greater accuracy than traditional methods and automatic validation of orders. Marketing should be involved in setting up these tools as there are many opportunities for increasing sales with appropriate upsell/cross-sell techniques. Relevant and useful product and solution collateral can also be added to educate sellers and customers when they browse your e-commerce sites.

Remember

- E-commerce sites complement the sales force, but it's important to address sales compensations and other concerns raised by the sales team.
- Articulate clearly how e-commerce will help the sales teams. For example: customers can order replacement parts directly online.
- Solicit sales feedback and input when designing e-commerce flows. Sales buy-in is critical.

Affiliate marketing

An affiliate marketing programme is a business arrangement whereby one party (the merchant or advertiser) agrees to pay another party (the affiliate or publisher) a referral fee, bounty or commission for every occurrence of a desirable action.[8] Examples of such actions include sales and leads or customers clicking on the affiliate's link prior to completing a sale. In many cases this manifests as affiliates and publishers who are driving traffic to your websites. Recently, affiliate marketing also expanded to cover influencer marketing such as bloggers and YouTube/Instagram celebrities. If you think about it, these so-called influencers are using their sites or social media channels to share and talk about your products and services, and in so doing are driving traffic to your site. Depending on how it's structured, affiliate or influencer marketing can easily be a paid sponsorship, a celebrity endorsement, a partner marketing effort or some other inbound channel. It comes in many different forms.

Affiliate marketing is undeniably becoming popular. A study of affiliate marketing trends by Forrester Consulting found that, as of 2016, more than 80 per cent of brands reported utilizing affiliate programmes, and they're contributing to what was predicted to be a $5.3 billion industry by the end of 2017. The study forecasts that the industry will experience growth in excess of 10 per cent each year through 2020, meaning that spending could rise to $6.8 billion in that time.[9]

In general, marketing teams work closely with affiliates to drive leads or sales. Affiliates or publishers will use typical marketing efforts such as email, paid search, social media, video, content publishing and issuing coupons to drive sales.

I love my accounting software, Xero. Its tagline is 'beautiful accounting software'. The design and user interface is simple and intuitive. Since they target small and medium businesses or small and medium enterprises in the US, Australia and the UK, lead generation is critical for their sales team. One of the key marketing activities is affiliate marketing. Xero's Affiliate Marketing Manager works closely with the company's affiliates to structure their programmes, from messaging, content creation, paid search keywords and email to other outbound efforts. Although he doesn't run the affiliates' marketing campaigns, it's important to set them up for success. In addition, he also spends time working on incentives and payouts. Since affiliate compensation is paid based on performance, incentives and payouts closely correlate with their behaviours. If affiliate marketing is optimized, it's as effective as channel partner marketing or other paid marketing efforts.

The impact of affiliate marketing on sales enablement

Affiliate marketing is not usually on the sales team's radar. However, with non-traditional affiliate partners as potential business development engines, sales teams may be interested in getting involved in identifying affiliate partners. For example, Reebok is working with CrossFit gyms to allow gym members to buy gear directly through the gym, which is then paid a commission on products sold through its Reebok storefront.[10]

Another element sales teams may find interesting is how affiliates position your products and services. To drive traffic to their sites, affiliates need to talk about your products slightly differently than your own company's messaging. It will be educational for you to see how they talk about your products and services. In addition, affiliates or influencers will conduct product reviews or comparisons. Some of the information can also be used by sales teams as talking points with prospects. Since some affiliates are influencers too, sales may be able to find prospects on influencers' social media channels, websites or their communities.

Many companies make the mistake of expecting affiliates to drive conversions while they sit back and watch the revenue pour in. The reality is that affiliate programmes are designed to bring traffic to your sites. No matter how they got there, it's *your* job to get customers who visit your site make a purchase. If your site is set up well, you'll drive more leads and sales, which in turn will increase the incentives you'll give your affiliates to boost their own contribution.

Affiliate marketing isn't exactly new. The concept has been around for a long time in the form of celebrity endorsements, but the digital revolution is giving everyday people a chance to get in on the action. Find influencers who are good brand advocates and offer them an opportunity to grow with you.

Remember

- Identify key affiliate programme partners and structured performance-based payout that both marketing and sales agree on. Modify and optimize as necessary.

- Create a seamless experience to facilitate affiliates' traffic to your site. Compare each affiliate's performance and adjust your budget.

- Work with affiliates to create differentiated messaging. Brief them well and provide information to help them succeed.

Loyalty programmes

Having a healthy business model is the be-all-and-end-all for every company. A strong team of sales associates does not do any good if your business cannot create repeat customers. Repeat customers are no good if the cost of retaining them outweighs the revenue they generate for the business.[11] One effective tactic is to create a loyalty or reward programme. US companies spend $50 billion a year on loyalty programmes alone. And if you get it right, loyalty programmes can generate as much as 20 per cent of a company's profits.[12] Loyalty or reward programmes are super-popular in B2C, especially in the travel, restaurant and retail segments. People join programmes because of the perks, complimentary services, discounts, cash back, rebates, status and other incentives.

As a rule, enterprise customers tend to build long-term and sustainable relationships with partners and suppliers. For B2B, the loyalty element can be hidden in other marketing programmes. For example: at one point, Intel had more than 200,000 channel partners worldwide. In order to better support different channel partners, Intel created tiered-level membership programmes and offered different membership benefits and rewards based on various levels of services and value (platinum, gold, silver status, etc). Membership benefits can include marketing support, attending invitation-only conferences, exclusive technical support, etc. Intel, Cisco, IBM and Microsoft all have their own proprietary channel partner conferences.

Loyalty programmes' impact on sales enablement

Data! The loyalty programme has most of your existing customers' demographic and purchase information. By looking at the data, you will understand your accounts' purchasing and usage habits. Even if you are not looking at specific customers, you can look at the data by specific segments or tiers to see if there are any consistent patterns. It's another way to get to know your customers well, which will help you provide better services.

Technology has played a major role in the evolution of loyalty programmes. For instance, smartphones can replace the loyalty card. SMS texting is replacing email for distributing digital coupons and offers. If loyalty email click activity is via mobile devices, then it is extremely important to optimize all digital marketing and e-commerce experiences for that format. The entire experience needs to be positive and not bogged down by poorly tuned web pages or apps.

The key to a successful loyalty and reward effort is making sure your customers feel valued for supporting your business. Customers who do not feel appreciated will spend their money elsewhere. Successful loyalty programmes analyse the profit customers generate and the influence they have more broadly on sales. The real payoff from loyalty programmes comes from locking in the customers who drive higher profitability.

Remember

- Understand the benefits of your company's loyalty programmes and share perks and benefits with prospects if it's a compelling talking point. Note: channel partner programmes may have some elements of loyalty programmes.
- Further comprehend buyer personas by correlating membership data from loyalty programmes and CRM.
- Technology plays a critical role in loyalty programmes. Smartphones can replace the loyalty card. SMS texting is replacing email for distributing digital product updates and offers.

Programmatic and retargeting ads

Retargeting, a form of online advertising, is served to people who have visited your website (pixel-based) or to contacts from your database (list-based). Pixel-based retargeting occurs when potential leads come to your website, a piece of JavaScript (known as a pixel) is placed on their browsers – making the browsers 'cookied'. When they leave your site to visit other sites, that cookie notifies retargeting platforms to serve specific ads based on the pages they visited on your website. List-based retargeting involves uploading a list of email addresses to a retargeting campaign (usually on social networks such as Facebook or Twitter) and the platform will identify users on that network who have those addresses and serve retargeting ads just to them.[13]

For most websites, only 2 per cent of web traffic converts on the first visit.[14] Retargeting is a tool that helps reach that 98 per cent of users who don't convert right away. There are plenty of upsides when it's done right. By displaying ads on other websites your leads visit, you can increase brand awareness, create virtual follow-up, and accelerate conversions. There are also plenty of downsides when it's not managed properly. We have all experienced non-stop ads that follow us around, which may damage the brand or even backfire, causing a reduction in the number of conversions.

The impact of retargeting on sales enablement

In the email marketing section above, Tom Martin shared examples of using behavioural email flows to identify warm and cold leads using an existing database. Similarly, you can also use list-based retargeting efforts to identify potential prospects in your database. The trick is to segment your database wisely and create ads with solid copy and crisp calls-to-action that are contextual to what your target is likely to be interested in.

If sales and marketing are working on account-based marketing, retargeting may be an option to build awareness before engaging with those accounts. Again, you may need to carefully craft your message and determine the appropriate frequency. You don't want to annoy potential leads.

Marketing Sherpa's Allison Banko published a great case study on retargeting. I received special permission from Marketing Sherpa's Senior Director, Daniel Burstein, to share excerpts from the case study. Lumension, a global leader in endpoint security software, devised a behavioural scoring model to discover the purchasing journey path that prospects were most likely to follow. Based on that, the marketing team focused their retargeting along that path: trial and evaluation, product and solution, information and pricing pages.[15] Lumension had since been merged with FrontRange and formed HEAT Software in 2015.[16]

When the company's marketing budget was cut by 30 per cent, the team needed to adjust its strategy to maintain their demand generation efforts. Lumension wanted to know if it was possible to expand its retargeting efforts to increase leads. At the same time, the team were clear they didn't want to implement a simple retargeting plan of 'Let's just have ads and follow people.' To begin, the marketing team took a look at the Lumension prospect base. From persona research, the team already knew who was searching for Lumension. They determined the company's sales cycle was six months, and there were three to five people involved in their purchase decision-making cycle. In other words, they were aware that multiple people within the same account often research the same topic. The team also realized that prospects were hitting multiple places on the internet to accomplish their research. They needed to determine how Lumension could reach them where they were searching. With that in mind, Ed Brice, VP of Marketing, had his team work with the company's media partners to help raise awareness of Lumension in that space. The team wanted to figure out how to take information they already had on prospects who had converted within the past five months to drive a personalized retargeting campaign to capture other similar prospects that did not convert. Lumension built a retargeting strategy on five key pillars:

1 Instant nurturing

2 Lead retargeting

3 Influencers

4 Behavioural intent look-alikes

5 Integrated online and offline event marketing and retargeting

1 Instant nurturing

This pillar addressed Lumension's direct leads, nurturing prospects with display ads immediately after they entered the funnel. By doing this, Lumension could 'follow' prospects as they continued their online journey based on the relevant information they provided. Key goals for the instant nurturing pillar included increasing sales cycle traction, recollection and conversions.

2 Lead retargeting

Lead retargeting encompassed contacts within the current prospect database who were either inactive or had previously opted out of Lumension's marketing automation campaigns. Based on previous page visits or offers they registered for, Lumension retargeted this set with specific creative display ads across the internet.

3 Influencers

From previous persona research, Lumension had determined that purchasing teams within the IT security space were comprised of three to five individuals. With the help of key media partners, the team could retarget contacts within the same company as the original lead. In addition, Lumension reached out to media partners to see if any of those prospects were landing in areas for which the partners were providing content. If so, Lumension asked if they could enable a retargeting campaign of display ads designed for individuals landing in those places.

4 Behavioural intent lookalikes

Working with media portals, the team retargeted contacts down-loading competitor content, but not Lumension assets. These are the people who were not yet fully engaged but were involved in a buying cycle within the IT security space. Through this tactic, Lumension could target companies that were in the market for IT security soft-ware but weren't in the company's funnel yet. Leveraging current target buyer information could drive behaviour lookalikes into Lumension's sales funnel.

5 Integrated online and offline event marketing and retargeting

'It's one of those classic cases of how we build a bridge between the offline world into the online world,' Brice stated. 'Within our industry, as with most other industries... there's always a handful of really big industry events.' One approach involved gating event coverage in media portals with Lumension ads to collect prospective contacts who had visited the Lumension booth. From there, the team matched booth visitors with those who were also on the roadblock pages. These folks were hit with a retargeting campaign designed exclusively for them.

Despite cutting their budget by 30 per cent, Lumension leveraged retargeting to increase total advertising impressions (leads) by 81 per cent and homepage views by 865 per cent. Lumension's total website traffic increased by 10 per cent, while its unique visitor traffic and page views both experienced an 8 per cent lift.

This case study showcases effective retargeting and how it works well as a complement to account-based selling. Doing it right is complicated, though. Marketing and their media partners need to really think strategically about the leads they want to focus on.

Lumension worked hard to identify five different categories of leads that they wanted to reach. Then, it's a matter of monitoring and optimizing. Use data to discover new targets.

> **Remember**
>
> - Retargeting complements account-based marketing.
> - Retargeting efforts needs to carefully consider who to retarget, as exemplified by Lumension's decision to focus on inactive accounts, influencers and look-alike customers.
> - Marketing needs to be actively involved and track retargeting performance, correlating results with that of the lead generation process and CRM data.

Social media marketing

Social media is also a 'must' for marketing. People share so much on social media. The platforms are becoming a social listening treasure trove to discover potential prospects' preferences and needs, both personally and professionally. Since almost everyone is on social media, you can also use those platforms as a channel to interact with your prospects and existing customers. In addition to conversing with their families and friends, people also recommend and refer products and services, turning the platform into a digital word-of-mouth referral service. Since people also praise or complain about brands, social media platforms can also serve as a customer-service outlet. As a marketer, you simply cannot ignore social media as part of your marketing strategy or marketing mix. As a salesperson, you also need to understand how to use social media to assist your sales efforts.

Here is a great example shared by Tom Martin. The sales team of a leading brand of whisky had been working hard to gain shelf space in targeted liquor stores in Texas. Martin and his agency team suggested a unique social media sales support programme. In order to gain more shelf space in these stores, the sales team communicated with the liquor store owners that the brand would run geo-targeted social media promoting free liquor tastings in their stores on agreed upon dates. These ads were designed to drive foot traffic to the stores where the goal was to have consumers purchase this particular whisky and any other liquor or mixers they might need. Ultimately, with increased foot traffic, they were able to convince the stores to give them more shelf space and increase year-over-year sales of the whisky by double, and in some instances triple, digit percentage growth. This is a great example of using social media as a sales tool to close deals.

The impact of social media on sales enablement

Many social media platforms are available. Salespeople need to spend time exploring and gaining an understanding of how and when to use each tool so they can determine the best ways to use social media as a creative sales tool that will show your customers what you can do for them.

- Social media is both a sales and marketing tool. As a salesperson, you need to understand how to use social media to assist your sales efforts.
- Work with marketing closely to craft customized social media marketing programmes as part of the sales deals.
- Social media marketing can also be part of account-based marketing.
- Marketing teams can prepare social media kits or set up relevant content on employee advocacy platforms.

Marketing programmes as your sales tool

Different marketing programmes can potentially be sales tools. The challenge of using marketing programmes creatively is that it requires a lot of time to plan and then work out the kinks during execution, which most salespeople are not interested in doing. They just want to receive solid leads from marketing and follow their regular routines to move leads through the buying phase with which they are familiar.

That attitude needs to change. Buyers are getting more sophisticated, and they also expect more from sellers.

In his book *The Three Value Conversations*, Erik Peterson said that sales reps are trained and conditioned to be problem-solvers for their customers. In addressing only 'known' problems, sellers are ceding control of the conversation to buyers. In a way, sales reps are putting themselves in what Erik calls the 'Commodity Box'. In order to turn the tables, you need to become a problem-finder, not a problem solver. 'The premium is your ability to tell buyers something useful about a problem or of a missed opportunity that they didn't even know they had.' The needs that buyers are not even considering are what he calls 'unconsidered needs.' Once you find the unconsidered needs, there are a lot of creative ways to drive those conversations. In addition to addressing technical issues, other creative solutions such as identifying additional partners, working on co-marketing, sharing tools or processes, and even sponsoring customers' events are approaches you can consider. Marketing programmes can be used as your sales tools.

Integrated marketing

Although I discussed each marketing programme separately, marketing has its maximum effect when each element is integrated into a comprehensive whole. When I discussed the Intel Inside campaign, it was coupled with partner marketing with key OEMs, ODMs and channel partners. For affiliates, driving traffic to your site involves multi-channel outreach efforts from sharing customer reviews, paid search, social media, video, content publishing, influencer outreach and more. As a marketer, it's important to have a holistic view of your company's marketing channels so that you determine which channels to use and when.

Ginger Shimp, Senior Marketing Director for SAP North America, has a challenging job. She needs to continue to strengthen SAP's thought leadership position while simultaneously delivering leads. In general, these two elements rarely overlap. One is related to top-of-the-funnel activities while the other focuses on bottom-of-the-funnel tactics. At the same time, because SAP has adopted an industry-led strategy, she also must drive demand for SAP's twenty-five verticals. What can she do to tie together both ends of funnels efficiently with one campaign and cover twenty-five verticals?

During her research she discovered a growing trend of business professionals listening to podcasts when they are on the road, at home, or even just taking a break. On average, Americans spend three hours and fifty-eight minutes each day consuming audio.[17] And podcast listening has grown steadily from 18 per cent in 2008 to 36 per cent in 2016.

Ginger's team decided to add podcasts as part of their influencer strategy. They contracted with the SMAC Talk (social, mobile, analytics, cloud) technology podcast, co-hosted by Dan Newman and Brian Fanzo, to create a podcast series comprised of episodes for each of the twenty-five verticals supported by SAP. She asked Dan and Brian to challenge the SAP executives. In some episodes, there were heated and passionate discussions about technology trends and products for any given industry. They kept the length to less than fifteen minutes, to produce something that people can consume quickly. It was a great way to build thought leadership, industry by industry, and thus it met two of Ginger's key objectives. But it didn't drive leads.

Ginger used content marketing to tackle her demand creation objective. She treated each podcast episode as a piece of long-form content and set up what she laughingly calls her 'digital chop shop'. By running each episode through a systematic digital-first process, Ginger and her team created snackable, socially sharable, digitally native content pieces that could be distributed on a multitude of outlets. They created blog posts for each episode to help with SEO. For Twitter, they produced a minimum of three Twitter cards for each episode. They went as far as creating audiograms to stream on Twitter. Executive-first PowerPoint presentations for each episode were a perfect fit for SlideShare. In addition, they created video content. They had captured video while recording the podcasts and used those to create a 'highlights' reel to post on YouTube. Naturally they syndicated episodes to various podcast outlets. On top of that, they did a paid media push as well as an email campaign.

A well-planned and thought-out promotional effort is really a demand generation campaign. Over 16,124 people listened to the episodes. They delivered 96,000 blog views with 5,300 blog referrals across twenty-five industries and two lines of business, and generated 43,078 unique contacts from 14,200 different companies, 3,600 inquiries, 125 sales qualified leads, and $23 million in pipeline from 107 opportunities.

Ginger didn't treat this specific podcast as a 'one and done' programme. She worked to ensure that all promotional efforts were integrated to give this programme a 125 per cent push. Although this is an influencer programme, in a way, this is also a form of paid sponsorship. And she further integrated content marketing, email marketing, social media marketing, and paid media to achieve maximum impact. Positioning the podcast to reach business professionals accomplishes the thought leadership objective. This allowed SAP's executives to share their expertise, which met the objective of covering all 25 verticals in SAP's portfolio and had the added benefit of appealing to listeners higher in the decision-making process. To drive demand, she used the episodes as a lead-in to get contact information from people who are interested in talking to SAP, positioning two ungated assets and one gated asset as the CTA (call to action) for each episode. The promotional effort became a lead gen catalyst.

At the peak of the Roman Empire, all roads led to Rome. When marketing is done right, all marketing leads to sales.

What you can do

1 Identify your company's marketing programmes that can be used as sales tools.

2 Find an opportunity in the sales pipeline that can be accelerated with marketing programmes.

3 Work with dedicated salespeople to explore and plan the above initiative.

Notes

1   Jack Trout. Peter Drucker on marketing. Forbes, 3 March 2006. www.forbes.com/2006/06/30/jack-trout-on-marketing-cx_ jt_0703drucker.html#602ef339555c

2   Walmart/Coke commercial *Stock up on joy*. www.youtube.com/ watch?v=AXXPIk4v6aw

3   Beth Snyder Bulik. Inside the Inside Intel campaign. Business Insider, 21 September 2009. www.businessinsider.com/inside-the-inside-intel-campaign-2009-9

4   Jonathan Crowe. How to avoid sales channel conflicts. Openview, 15 April 2018. https://labs.openviewpartners.com/how-to-avoid-sales-channel-conflict/#.WmEptpM-duV

5   Tom Martin. *The Invisible Sale: How to build a digitally powered marketing and sales system to better, prospect, qualify, and close leads.* Que Publishing, Indianapolis. 2013

6   Maria Aspan. Mailchimp, Company of the Year. *Inc. Magazine*, Winter 2017/2018

7   Blue Sky Technology Partner. Sales enablement: 5 essentials for B2B e-commerce. Blue Sky Technology Partner Blog, 4 December 2015. www.blueskytp.com/sales-enablement-e-commerce-roi

8   Evgenii Geno Prussakov. *Affiliate Program Management: An hour a day.* Sybex, Canada, 2011

9   Rhett Power. Increase sales with an affiliate program that works. Inc. 21 November 2017. www.inc.com/rhett-power/increase-sales-with-an-affiliate-marketing-program-that-works.html

10 Mike [n.s]. Strategic partnership for your crossfit gym using affiliate and referral marketing. The Box Business. http://theboxbusiness.com/strategic-partnerships-crossfit-gym-using-affiliat

11 Liz Bedor. How New York & Company's loyalty program drives 40% of sales. www.bluecore.com/blog/new-york-company-loyalty-programs

12 Tariq Shaukat and Phil Auerbach. Loyalty: Is it really working for you? www.mckinsey.com/business-functions/marketing-and-sales/our-insights/loyalty-is-it-really-working-for-you

13 Dan Hecht. A beginner's guide to retargeting ads. Hubspot, 5 September 2017. https://blog.hubspot.com/marketing/retargeting-campaigns-beginner-guide.

14 ReTargeter.com. What is retargeting and how does it work? https://retargeter.com/what-is-retargeting-and-how-does-it-work

15 Allison Banko. B2B retargeting: How Lumension achieved 865% lift in homepage view. Marketing Sherpa, 30 July 2014. www.marketingsherpa.com/article/case-study/b2b-retargeting-increase-homepage-visits

16 Helen Carroll. FrontRange and Luemnsion to merge and form HEAT software. Ivanti, 15 February 2015. www.ivanti.com/company/press-releases/2015/frontrange-and-lumension-to-merge-and-form-heat

17 The Podcast Consumer. www.edisonresearch.com/wp-content/uploads/2016/05/The-Podcast-Consumer-2016.pdf

Design and user experience enhance sales success

07

What is the best user experience for a shovel? Answer: a hole.
AZA RASKIN

Ease-of-use design has been elevated by the prevalence of small form-factor devices such as smartphones, tablets, digital watches and Internet of Things (IoT) devices. Although the design of hardware is important, the user experience offered by software plays an even more prominent role in influencing end-users' purchase decision. In some cases, the ease-of-use benefits are a key component of the value proposition that differentiates you from your competitors.

Ever since he was in college in the late 1980s, a friend of mine, Larry, has been a die-hard Apple user. In the 1980s most applications, especially games, were built and tailored for a PC running Microsoft Windows. For university work, and eventually his job, Larry would use a PC like everyone else. And he would play games on his PC, too. Yet, there was always a Mac in his room. Deep down, despite the need to use a PC for mainstream applications, Larry holds Apple dear to his heart. I asked him why he switched back and forth, despite the extra work it required. Why didn't he just stick to one system and let Apple go? I still remember his reply vividly: 'With Apple, every-thing' – then he paused and shouted – '*just works*! And its design is intuitive.'

Like most people of my generation, I was a Windows user for over twenty years. Apple never really entered my life until I purchased my first iPhone. With the iPhone, naturally, I wanted to integrate the content in my phone with my computer. I decided to buy a MacBook in 2011. It took me two or three weeks to get familiar with Apple's user interface. Once I understood the lie of the land, I agreed with Larry. It just works. I remember my husband asked me to download something for him using his PC several weeks after I purchased my MacBook. When I turned on his PC, my mind went completely blank for about five minutes and I forgot where I should click or what I should do to download a simple file. How quickly I forgot! I was looking at the PC as if I had never used it before. I wouldn't say that I love my PC, but I'd say that I love my Mac. Its design leads to a superb user experience. I finally understand what people mean when they say it's intuitive.

The ease of use and intuitiveness has been further validated by babies and toddlers. A team of researchers at the University of Iowa studied more than 200 YouTube videos and concluded that 90 per cent of the children in the videos had a moderate ability to use a tablet by age two.[1] They have no training on computers or keyboards, yet they can just pick up an iPad and make magic happen by swiping, pointing or tapping icons on screens with their tiny fingers. Again, the design is so intuitive that, somehow, they just *know* what to do. But making usage easy is hard work. Behind the curtain, it's a group of designers doing extensive research, testing numerous wireframes and mock-ups, making agonizing trade-offs and working through kinks and back-end challenges to hide the complexities from users. In the business world, we talk about products needing to have a competitive advantage or unique differentiator. The core of Apple's competitive advantage or unique differentiator is *design*, in addition to making hardware and software working together.

For software design, ease of use is as important as functionality. People who are used to simple intuitive designs won't tolerate unfriendly or difficult-to-navigate applications. The dominance of iPhones and iPads has elevated the role of design and the user interface. The ramifications of that have spread to other consumer electronics and goods, store layouts, furniture, even medical devices and more. Design is front-and-centre and as important as content, workflow, functionality, layout, and components. Design transforms the experience. And the experience matters in the digital age.

Quantify ROI of design and user experience

We all know user experience matters, but it's almost impossible to tie the design directly to revenue growth. Ken Chizinsky, Senior Manager of User Experience for the Digital Sales Strategy and Design Team at Cisco, and his team were responsible for designing the highly popular Cisco SalesConnect software used by the direct sales team and indirect sales force. He addressed the question of whether it was possible to tie design and user experience to sales revenue.

> When we designed SalesConnect, we made an effort to emphasize metrics. We wanted to measure the impact of this platform. SalesConnect has a high adoption rate. We can measure the content pieces that are most consumed, the users who consumed them, the length of time spent on the content, and even keyword searches and more. But we can't correlate sales with design yet.

Ken and his team, however, are exploring the use of big data to run regression or statistical analysis to determine if specific personalization features on the platform can drive better efficiency for the sales team by saving users time and energy. Even though SalesConnect's design ROI cannot be quantified, Cisco's senior management are committed to continually improving the tool. After all, the high adoption rate indicates that direct and indirect sales teams are using the tool to find relevant content and facilitate customers' meetings and engagements.

The role of user experience in assisting sales

A user experience designer's job has historically been limited to product and website design. Verne Lindner, Senior User Experience (UX) Architect of Puppet, has been working closely with software engineers to design Puppet's products. Founded in 2005, and in use at over 40,000 companies, Puppet provide tools to help IT and system administrators manage system configuration. As a UX designer, Verne has worked on keynote demos with product leadership and on support materials for demos and customer-facing literature. She feels strongly that UX can and should help the sales team design effective and user-friendly demos. User experience designers need to begin focusing their value-add services to enable the sales team and not just product teams. A UX designer's knowledge on product and website design can easily lend a hand to create effective and user-friendly sales product demo designs and tie the overall experience among product, sales demos and online experience all together.

As a sales representative, you need to understand that design and experience plays a role in helping you to sell. This chapter will explore design and user experience in the context of sales engagements and processes by focusing on the following four topics:

- incorporating interactive content into sales processes and training
- including sales messages inside SaaS-based products or company apps
- sourcing user-friendly sales enablement tools
- creating intuitive and buyer-focused marketing communications

Incorporating interactive content into sales processes and training

Most of the content we see today is two-dimensional (2D). Some 2D content includes interactive elements that require customers to enter information or answer questions by completing surveys, responding to quizzes or engaging with ROI or cost savings calculators. You may have seen interactive and animated home pages, infographics, ebooks, videos and other formats. As long as the content is digital, you can work with your technical teams to make it fun and engaging. You can even turn your content into a mini-movie if you are creative and ambitious enough, but that's a budget discussion.

With the rise of augmented reality (AR) and virtual reality (VR), we can now make 2D three-dimensional, creating an experience in which your customers virtually feel and touch your products. Augmented reality means projecting virtual information on top of the real world.[2] The best-known AR example is the popular game Pokémon Go and companies such as Ikea, the Swedish furniture retailer, have done a great job in incorporating this technology into their mobile apps. Check out the YouTube video 'Place Ikea furniture in your home with augmented reality'.[3] Virtual reality means complete immersion in another world, blocking out the real world. A good example is Google Earth VR. You can fly around the planet like Superman, exploring locations from above using an Oculus Rift or HTC Vive headset[4] (Google is actively exploring support for other platforms).[5] You can drop down to ground level to explore Street View imagery from 85 countries using the Google Earth VR app, which I experienced using a friend's HTC Vive. It is amazing. When you have a chance, please try it. Mixed reality (MR) means placing artificial information and objects positionally and rotationally correct into 3D space in real time. If graphic designers create animated characters on their computers, they can instantly project the image into 3D space in real time. The most famous example is Microsoft's Hololens technology. We refer to this group of technologies as cross reality, or xR.

The xR realm is poised to have a massive impact not only on consumers, but also on sales and marketing. Rather than showing an image or sharing a spec sheet, what about bringing the products to life and letting your customers virtually touch, feel, test and experience them? Caterpillar sell large equipment in industries such as mining, construction, energy and transportation. It's challenging to bring the physical equipment to a client site for a demo.[6] According to Terri Lewis, Digital and Technology Director at Caterpillar, her team are working hard to leverage AR and VR in all aspects of sales, operations and service applications.

> The company have already created a tractor in a virtual reality app that includes 6,000 part numbers. A salesperson could use an iPhone or iPad to hover over an icon on a specifications sheet to have a virtual rendering of the product pop-up as a visual. Or, on the job site, you could do a simulation of digging trenches to see if it would violate any requirements for highway control, for example.

That's what sales demos should look like; the ability to demonstrate products in real time and let the clients see the benefits instantly. The demos may also help salespeople identify 'unconsidered needs' by letting customers experience the products and view the design or specifications in 3D. A well-done 3D xR experience can stimulate an adrenaline surge and trigger a buying impulse that may accelerate the buying cycle from your customers.

Applying xR technologies to sales and other aspects of business is new for everyone. Lewis shared her lessons learned:

7.1

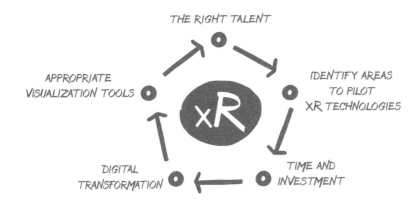

- Talent in xR is hard to find. You need to find someone who understands control systems and knows how to put the data into a 3D format so that people can interact with it. This person needs to be both creative and technical.

- Identify areas to pilot xR technologies. Ultimately, the goal of any xR implementation is to make money. Use technology to solve either internal challenges or customers' issues.

- The time and investment required to create, test and deploy xR are still prohibitive for many companies. The cost needs to go down tremendously before it will scale widely.

- Digitize equipment, components, drawings, specifications, other products and related information. It takes time to make that digital transformation. You'll also need to pull in sensor data to create that realistic experience. These are the fundamental prerequisites.

- Some visualization tools are not adapted to harsh environments. Headset, smartphones and glasses are options, but you need to determine what works well for you.

Two YouTube videos shared by Caterpillar can give you a good sense how xR technologies assist in showcasing products to deliver a better user experience: 'Caterpillar augmented and virtual reality'[7] and 'Caterpillar's CAVE virtual reality system'.[8]

The impact of xR technologies on sales enablement

Development in xR is progressing at lightning speed. Just like the ramp of the telephone, television, personal computers and smartphones, the technology and pricing will need to hit a tipping point to induce mass adoption. Several phone manufacturers are working hard to add 3D to their smartphones' video recording capabilities. Maybe that can be one of the tipping points to drive 3D adoption in the future.

What marketers and sales teams need to understand is that 3D content will become part of the overall sale and marketing content mix. The key is to understand how different aspects of xR may impact sales enablement.

Product

You can provide product simulations, showcase worst case scenarios and conduct root cause analysis. xR also offers buyers a 'try before you buy' experience. You can use it to perform virtual focus group testing and use the feedback to further improve both the product and the overall xR experience. A great example is Merrell's launch of their most innovative hiking shoes via TraiScape, a four-dimensional (4D) multisensory hiking experience that allows customers wearing the shoes to try different surfaces and obstacles, such as rockslides.[9] Check out the highlights in the YouTube video 'Merrell "Trailscape", Framestore VR Studio'.[10]

Training

xR can also apply to interactive training, role playing and situational conversation simulations. It can be a valuable aid for teaching salespeople how to use products, especially complicated products. xR-based self-paced training and 3D 'living manuals' offer a richer and more effective method of educating people on new products and processes.

Maintenance and operations

xR can also support the automation of manufacturing processes, field service, maintenance and repairs. By using augmented reality overlays to assist in troubleshooting and operations of complex equipment, a technician can be guided through required steps more efficiently. Data captured from xR can then be used to help optimize maintenance and operations. In turn, salespeople can share the lessons learned with customers to assist their maintenance and operations, further cementing the relationship.

Sales and marketing

Lowe's, a major home improvement and appliance store in the US, created Lowe's Holoroom, which is a virtual reality home improvement design and visualization tool that empowers homeowners with an immersive, intuitive experience in the room of their dreams. It started as a concept from Lowe's innovation lab, then rolled out to different stores. Since xR is still evolving, the innovation lab continues to use new technology, and customer and employee feedback to refine and improve the holoroom. See 'Lowe's innovation labs – the next-generation Lowe's holoroom'.[11]

BMW offers virtual test-drives with their new i8 and i3 models. Using a mobile app, you can configure your ideal vehicle, then perform a virtual test drive. It's not 100 per cent xR, but BMW made an effort to create an immersive experience. See 'BMW, become electric – a virtual reality experience'.[12]

Another example is from Villeroy & Boch, premium European manufacturers of porcelain, ceramic, wellness and tableware products, who created an augmented reality app to assist customers with their purchase of bathroom furniture and appliances. The app projects Villeroy & Boch products into a user's bathroom from multiple angles to give a realistic visualization of what they will look like before purchase. You can even see the placement in different degrees of sunlight. The app overview is displayed in the video 'Augmented reality app (EN) – Villeroy & Boch'.[13]

Multiple car brands have been using xR to let potential buyers experience test drives using their mobile phone along with goggles and other devices. As the technology matures and production costs decrease, more brands will test the water using xR technologies to help their customers 'experience' their products by merging the real and virtual worlds moving forward.

In the xR realm, sales and marketing communications need to be subtle. Nobody wants to be bombarded with blatant retargeting ads in VR or AR. Marketers need to discern user preferences and place discreet, well-thought-out objects into the overall experience. xR has the potential to transform sales tactics, sales training, or even sales organizations to offer the ultimate sales experience. Sales management needs to determine how best to leverage xR in the future to further the team's growth and productivity.

Remember

- Understand the differences between AR, VR and MR technologies.
- Be aware of the challenges of piloting and implementing xR technologies. You may not see the ROI immediately.
- Comprehend xR technologies' impact on product development, maintenance, operations, sales and marketing. We are only limited by our own imagination.

Including sales messages within SaaS-based products or company apps

Software has come a long way. In the past, we purchased software in a package, then used the CD (or floppy disk) inside that box to install the software on a computer. Today, many applications are sold as a service that you pay for on a subscription basis, which is called software as a service (SaaS). The software is hosted in the cloud and we mainly access it via the internet or sometimes download applications or plugins locally on the device being used. There are a growing number of SaaS examples, including Google Gmail, Microsoft Office 365, Adobe Creative Cloud, GoToMeeting, Salesforce.com, DocuSign, Dropbox, Slack and many more.

Since the SaaS companies own their software designs and user interfaces, they can easily incorporate demand generation and sales components into their SaaS products as part of the overall experience. Zoom is a popular SaaS-based video communications platform for audio and video conferencing, chat, webinars and screen sharing. After you sign up and before starting to use Zoom, it discreetly displays an 'invite colleagues' option with clever copy such as 'Don't zoom alone.' In an effort to increase the user base, Zoom prompts you to help your friends and colleagues by suggesting their useful toolsets. It's a digital form of word-of-mouth.

Uberconference, another SaaS-based conferencing tool, adds a marketing text to the bottom of the account setting menu. 'Do you love Uberconference? Try Dialpad – modern business voice, video and messaging.' This message encourages cross-sales of other products in a company. Of course, because this is a digital/online platform it can swap its messages at any time.

Norton Internet Security, which produces antivirus and security SaaS-based software packages, has a 'message' menu item in their cloud-based software. Among other uses, they send messages to their subscribers about new features, tips and offerings. At the very beginning of the year, I received a message: 'Check out the top 5 digital safety tips for 2018.' When Meltdown and Spectre, two processor-based vulnerabilities affecting nearly every operating system and device, hit the mainstream media, Norton Security used the message feature to notify customers with a 'Security alert: Meltdown and Spectre.' In addition to explaining what Meltdown and Spectre are, it also reminds users to 'make sure all system patches are installed and your Norton is up to date on all PCs, Macs, and mobile devices' with a strong call-to-action, 'Protect more devices', which should drive additional purchases. In effect, this is email marketing that is embedded within the product itself and a great example of the embedding marketing outreach mechanism within Norton's SaaS-based product being used to respond to customers' needs and maximize marketing opportunities.

Another SaaS-based collaboration service, Podio, offer a web-based platform for organizing team communications, business processes, data and content in project management workspaces. To encourage users to try different features inside Podio, they designed a bulletin board-like space labelled 'There are things to explore…' It provides features and tips that you should try.

If you do a lot of video recording on your laptop, I'd suggest that you look into Loom, a cloud-based video recording platform. Even though the design is user-friendly and intuitive, users still need a bit of ramp time to get up-to-speed on the tool. So it created an onboarding checklist for new users. It walks you virtually through the stages of 'recording your video', 'customize a video', 'share a video' and 'get your first view'. Once you complete the checklist, you know how to make a basic video recording using Loom. Since it adds new features constantly, it includes a 'Product roadmap' as part of the tool so that you can see what features have been added lately. It's interesting to see that the customer onboarding is digitalized, which has an impact on the overall purchase journey.

User experience and design play an important role for e-commerce as well. Amazon is one of the most prevalent examples of an e-commerce company. Amazon's design and experience is not the most beautiful, but it is the most functional. They understand that users want to browse, and they facilitate that by showing similar items. Every time you add an item to your virtual shopping cart, Amazon display other items that are 'frequently bought together'. Also, the key to their success is that they combine the online shopping experience with seamless offline returns. Amazon makes sure the workflow is simple and hide the complicated back-end technology from their customers. In that sense, they take a similar approach to Apple.

There are countless other examples of SaaS-based products cleverly incorporating marketing communications, customer services, and sales elements. Training, customer onboarding, post sales, cross-selling and even customer surveys can be a seamless part of the products too. Adding these features to companies' SaaS-based platforms has ramifications on overall sales tactics and processes.

In order to continue to grow, these companies constantly add new features to maintain their unique advantages in the fiercely competitive landscape. Often, these features also become differentiators for tier-pricing and segmentation of customers ranging from individuals, small businesses, mid-size companies to enterprises. It's interesting to see how features define pricing, customer segmentation and, ultimately, sales tactics and engagements. Selling SaaS-based products is also different from traditional technology selling. Winning by Design specializes in transforming sales groups of SaaS companies. Its founder, Jacco van der Kooij, wrote a useful book, *Blueprint: SaaS methodology*.[14] In it, he discusses SaaS sales processes, sales models, structure of teams and most importantly, pricing and cost analysis for SaaS products. It's a great read if you are interested in SaaS selling, sales segmentation, pricing and cost analysis.

Remember

- User experience and design come first.
- Understand how sales and marketing elements can be incorporated seamlessly into SaaS-based platforms, e-commerce, community, company websites or mobile apps.

Sourcing user-friendly sales enablement tools

There is a great opportunity afforded by new and constantly improving technology but, even if you know what you are looking for, wading through the large number of offerings and tools can be extremely difficult. Scott Brinker, Program Chair at Martech Conference, compiled an infographic of the 2017 'marketing technology landscape' (technologies related to sales are also included) to track the number of companies in marketing technology since 2011. He listed only 150 companies in 2011. In 2017 he captured 4,891 companies with 5,381 solutions in six categories: advertising and promotion, content and experience, social and relationships, commerce and sales, data, and management.[15] He called it 'martech 5000'. Brinker noted the interesting distribution of the companies' size and funding:

- 6.9 per cent are enterprises with more than 1,000 employees or are public

- 44.2 per cent are private businesses with fewer than 1,000 employees or no funding data
- 48.8 per cent are investor-funded start-ups at any pre-exit stage

'Essentially, this market is a "long tail" distribution of marketing technology (martech) companies: a few $1+ billion giants, dozens of leaders with $100 million or more in revenue, and then THOUSANDS of smaller firms — from 1–3-person micro-SaaS companies to substantial firms with millions in revenue.'

Like Intel, Microsoft and other original equipment manufacturers working tirelessly to build the PC ecosystem, most major martech players such as Salesforce.com and Amazon embrace the ecosystem by making it easy for other vendors to build plugs-ins for their more specialized and vertical solutions. End-users can integrate plugs-in as they see fit. Although martech companies build plug-ins for easy integration, they make an effort to downplay that and position themselves as a 'one stop shop' or 'end-to-end solution'.

On one spectrum, most companies' sales and marketing technology stacks are centred around CRM, marketing automation platform and content management system. These are central repositories of data and services that other solutions will plug into. On the other end of the spectrum from the central repositories is the integration-platform-as-a-service (iPaaS). It connects to all the various cloud services (such as Salesforce.com, Hubspot, etc) and pulls data from each of those systems. The data is then normalized and delivered in a single, comprehensive interface.[16] For example, marketing professionals may need go to various tools to collect, store, analyse and report on their lead generation efforts, customer satisfaction surveys, website analytics and more. An iPaaS would take the data from all of these different cloud-based and on-premise solutions and integrate it into one single set of data. The data can then be accessed through a single interface.

It does not matter if your company uses a more centralized or decentralized approach; you still need some sort of 'sales enablement' tools to support you in the digital era. If you lead a sales enablement team or manage a virtual team, you need to look at 'sales enablement' as a whole to determine a stack of tools best suited for your teams. If you are an individual contributor as a sales enablement person, you need to determine what tools you need to do your job. Most sales enablement tools on the market focus on sales. In addition to CRM, there are tools for productivity, email tracking, social selling, sales intelligence, relationship building, content management, collaboration, training and more.

As a marketer supporting the sales team, you can choose to use their tools or purchase a new tool. If the tool is for your own use and the sales team does not need to learn another tool, by all means select and pick the tools that work for you. If the sales team need to use the tool, you need to make sure that you have a solid reason why they need to learn a new tool and how it will help them. You will also need to secure executive support to ensure the tool is used. You know how excited (or frustrated) salespeople can be if they need to spend time learning new tools. In addition to marketing automation tools and CRM tools, more and more sales teams are implementing sales enablement platforms such as Highspot, Engagio, Fusion Grove, Azaleads, Veelo and more. In order to entice the sales team to use them, the tools need to be intuitive and serve their needs. A good sales enablement tool should be able to effectively aid seller-to-buyer communication and enhance their connection during the sales cycle.

With a wealth of platforms to choose from, many organizations find it difficult to decide which sales enablement tool is best for their business. However, there are several key factors to consider when analysing which solution to invest in.[17]

7.2

EASE OF USE | INTEGRATION

CONTENT MANAGEMENT | MOBILE READINESS | ANALYTICS

- **Ease of use:** First and foremost, the tool you choose should be relatively easy to use and understand. Of course, any new piece of software requires training, and this should be carried out team-wide by someone who is proficient in using it. However, the platform as a whole should be straightforward. Happily, many sales enablement tools offer trial versions, so you can get a good sense of their fit for your use.

- **Integration:** Above all, whichever platform you choose must seamlessly integrate with the sales tools you use every day. Customer relationship management is the backbone of sales, so the tool you select needs to integrate successfully with it, without compromising data security, data storage and other important aspects. When doing your research, be sure to compare how each tool works with your CRM, social selling tools, the cloud and your email host. Ideally, this will be achievable all in one place. If integration is not fast and convenient, your sales team may not use it.

- **Content management:** According to the Chief Marketing Officer Council, 40 per cent of a B2B sales representative's time is spent searching for or creating content for new prospects, thus wasting a lot of valuable time. Overcoming this problem is easy when the team has access to a sales enablement tool that allows them to create a strong content knowledge base and archive. Without access to the right content at the right time, a sales team will nearly always fail. As such, any good sales enablement tool will be able to deliver relevant content when it is needed. This includes lead generation content such as case studies and white papers; internal sales support content such as product sheets, competitor analyses and sales scripts; and sales conversion content such as email templates and slide decks.

- **Mobile readiness:** In a mobile-first world, any software you choose should certainly be able to deliver sales content easily to any mobile device. Sales teams are always on the move and will constantly use their smartphones to access their CRM and other essential tools, so applications must have a mobile-aware interface.

- **Analytics:** There is simply no point in investing in software if you cannot see whether it is adding value to your business and helping you to achieve your goals. Always be sure to look for platforms that are able to provide data and reports on both customer insights and internal staff usage. For example, a good sales enablement tool will be able to provide reports on which content is getting viewed the most, how the sales team are using the content, and what the ROI is.

Here are some steps you can take to source sales enablement tools.

- **Define company goals:** There are countless tools on the market and each has its own strengths. Some will be best for content management, while others will be better at guiding the team through each stage of the sales process. You need to think about what your goals are and what you seek to improve within your current strategy – only then will you be able to find the best solution for your specific business needs.

- **Conduct needs analysis:** Determine what you want the software to do. Why do you need it? What do you want to accomplish? What is impeding sales performance? Can you purchase new modules or features from existing software to address the same issue?

- **Check existing sales tools:** You may have a list of tools already in use. Take an inventory of these tools and seek feedback on what works and what doesn't. Also, maybe new modules or features for some of your existing tools can be added to address your needs. You should also consider what tools can be retired, and the potential cost savings.

There are hundreds of sales enablement platforms out there. They all have different niches and solve different sales challenges. Knowing what you are looking for will guide the tool sourcing.

- **Identify potential tools:** Conduct research to narrow down the tool list. Depending on the complexity of tools, you may be able to do free trials or testing. Depending on the scope, you could hire a consulting firm to help with the selection.

- **Select the tool and track usage:** Once the tool is selected, it's important to train users and ensure the tool is being used. At the end of the day, tools are here to make your job easier.

It is helpful to have a holistic view of where the tools you are considering fit into the overall martech technology stack. Here are two links to examples of Microsoft and Cisco attempting to show how their and others' technologies and platforms fit into the sales journey:

bit.ly/koganpagedidner1   bit.ly/koganpagedidner2

The two images show a holistic view of various marketing and sales technologies needed at the pre-sale, sales and post-sales stages of the purchase journey. If you are overwhelmed with the types of vendors or technologies at each stage, these two images provide a good overview that may help start your preliminary research for specific tools.

Remember

- Have a holistic view of where the tools you are considering fit into the overall martech technology stack.

- Identify key selection criteria before sourcing tools: ease-of-use, integration, content management, mobile-readiness, analytics.

Creating intuitive and buyer-focused marketing communications

I had a conversation with a digital marketing director who was leading the website and e-commerce redesign of an electronic equipment company. The company manufactures testing and measurement devices for different industries. When I talked to him, he had just come out of the e-commerce site design and timeline review with his CEO. He was frustrated and discouraged. When he presented the e-commerce timeline, from design to implementation, his CEO couldn't understand why it would take so long. From the CEO's perspective, an e-commerce site is just a website with all the product images and descriptions, then you add 'Buy' buttons for each product and build a payment flow. That's it. Why would it be difficult? It should not take more than three months to build. The marketing director had a hard time convincing his CEO otherwise.

On the surface, the CEO seems to be right. When you go to every e-commerce site, you see products, product descriptions, then you add your items to a cart, then you pay. That's how we shop on Amazon. We search for what we need, we find it, then we make the purchase. Shouldn't we follow the same flow for B2B transactions? What the CEO failed to comprehend is that professional buyers don't make decisions quickly. When business buyers browse, they don't buy immediately. They need to gather information, do research, make comparisons, form a committee, conduct vendor reviews... There are considerations that buyers have before they hit that buy button. When an e-commerce site is built, the designer needs to take into account the different stages of the purchase journey that customers may be in, then sprinkle relevant content in different areas to encourage clicks and viewing. Beautiful product images, crisp product descriptions and a user-friendly payment flow are easy to set up. The challenging part is to add relevant information and content to your design and layout, anticipating customers' needs and questions. Building that 'experience' into your site takes time and effort to do well.

REI (Recreational Equipment, Inc.), outdoor adventure retailers in the US, sell camping gear, travel equipment, sporting goods, and outdoor attire. When they redesigned their e-commerce website, they defined their website objective as: 'Recreating the offline shopping experience online.' This is the mentality you should have when you explore design and user experience online. What kind of experience do you want to share with your users?

Design needs to drive sales. Certain sales-focused elements need to be seamlessly incorporated into various pages and places. 'Contact us' or 'Freephone/Toll free number' need to be prominent, usually in the upper right-hand corner (for western users). Many websites incorporate chat windows, which are similar to the automatic answering services employed by credit card or airline companies. Some of these chat windows are managed by bots, some of them are managed by humans with specific office hours. When users view a demo, it may be fitting and proper to add a 'contact us' button right next to the demo. Consider why customers view specific types of content. If they view awareness-based content, should you serve them more content that will help them understand your products better? If they view a demo, should you ask them if they would like to 'contact us'? Anticipate what customers will do on the specific page and usher them to the next step of the purchase cycle.

Your website or e-commerce site is your hub, destination and home base. It's your sale enablement tool. Outbound communications are aimed at driving traffic to your website. In addition, the site is also where you will gather leads. Therefore, creating an intuitive and buyer-focused website is essential. A well-designed website is the marketing team's secret weapon to generate more qualified leads for their sales teams.

In their book *The Heart of Change*, John Kotter and Dan Cohen state that most people believe change happens in this order: Analyse → Think → Change. 'But in reality, they say, the sequence of change in almost all successful change efforts actually looks more like See → Feel → Change.'[18] The design and user experience are intended to help your customer turn on their right brain to see, feel, then buy.

Apple spoils all of us with the mentality of 'It just works'. Everyone expects everything to 'just work'. Salespeople expect tools to just work and be intuitive. Customers expect your products to just work. Optimization of design and user experience is a never-ending journey.

Remember

- Design can drive sales. Certain sales-focused elements need to be seamlessly incorporated into various pages and places to increase conversions.

- The design and user experience, if done right, will help your customers to turn on their right brain to see, feel then buy.

What you can do

1 Explore working with a user experience designer to create or refine a sales demo to be more interactive, even possibly leveraging VR or AR.

2 Identify any opportunities to incorporate clever and seamless sales or marketing messages into your website, apps or SaaS products.

3 Reassess your existing sales enablement tools to understand the user experience for your sales team and how it might be improved, either with additional features, or even by a new tool.

Notes

1 Mark Prigg. The iPad really is child's play: More than half of toddlers can use Apple tablet when they are just one. Dailymail. com, 3 July 2015. www.dailymail.co.uk/sciencetech/article-3149025/ The-iPad-really-child-s-play-half-toddlers-use-Apple-s-tablet-just-ONE-researchers-say.html

2 Joerg Osarek. *Virtual Reality Analytics: How VR and AR change business intelligence*, Goordon's Arcade, Bad Homburg, Germany, 2016

3 Place Ikea furniture in your home with augmented reality. www. youtube.com/watch?v=vDNzTasuYEw

4 Trevor Mogg. Google Earth VR now lets you explore Street View imagery from 85 countries. Digital Trends, 16 September 2017. www. digitaltrends.com/virtual-reality/google-earth-vr-street-view

5 Adi Robertson. You can now fly around Google Earth in virtual reality. The Verge, 16 November 2016. www.theverge. com/2016/11/16/13643550/google-earth-vr-htc-vive-release

6 Stephanie Neil. Caterpillar's augmented reality. Automation World, 23 May 2017. www.automationworld.com/article/industry-type/all/ caterpillars-augmented-reality

7 Modernidade Digital. Caterpillar augmented and virtual reality. www.youtube.com/watch?v=lAEOgW_KeQA

8 Caterpillar's CAVE virtual reality system. www.youtube.com/watch? v=r9N1w8PmD1E

9 Caoimhe Gaskin. 7 examples of successful virtual reality marketing. Digital Marketing Institute, 19 January 2018. https://digitalmarketinginstitute.comblog/2018-01-19-7-examples-of-successful-virtual-reality-marketing

10 Merrell 'Trailscape', Framestore VR Studio. www.youtube.com/watch?v=efd6WhPmTyU

11 Lowe's innovation labs – the next-generation Lowe's holoroom. www.youtube.com/watch?time_continue=87&v=DVsEb9vla-I

12 BMW, become electric – a virtual reality experience. www.youtube.com/watch?v=3dtY7umPlDY

13 Augmented reality app (EN) – Villeroy & Boch. www.youtube.com/watch?v=CWC8aL6UKwE

14 Jacco Van der Kooij and Fernando Pizarro. *Blueprint: SaaS methodology*, CreateSpace Independent Publishing Platform, 2017

15 Scott Brinker. Marketing technology landscape supergraphic. Chief Martech, 10 May 2017. https://chiefmartec.com/2017/05/marketing-techniology-landscape-supergraphic-2017

16 Adrian Mott. SaaS vs. iPaaS: Understanding the difference! Bedrock Data. www.bedrockdata.com/blog/saas-versus-ipaas-understanding-the-difference

17 Jason Liu. How to choose the right sales enablement tool for your business. Sales Pop, 1 September 2017. https://salespop.pipelinersales.com/sales-management/how-to-choose-the-right-sales-enablement-tool-for-your-business

18 John Kotter and Dan Cohen. *The Heart of Change: Real life stories of how people change their organizations*, Harvard Business Review Press, 2012

When it's time to build your sales enablement team

Sales enablement is about preparing the sales team.
BOYD DAVIS, CEO OF KOGENTIX

Although I am writing this book from a marketer's perspective, this specific chapter will look at the structure of a sales enablement team from a more holistic perspective, not just from a marketer's point of view. A sales enablement team structure is fluid and every company does it differently. Some companies don't have a clearly identified sales enablement team. If you dive deeper, you can see that sales enablement functions do exist, but they are parsed out across different departments. They use processes and tools to tie everything together so that sales teams get what they need. Some companies have a sales enablement programme manager who serves as the main point of contact for the sales teams. This person's job is to work closely with other groups within the company to better support sales. Some companies have a formal and dedicated sales enablement team with a budget, tools and processes in place, but they still have to work closely with other functions to design training, content and other related sales enablement tactics.

In order to provide concrete recommendations, I spoke to several vice presidents or directors of sales and sales operations as well as sales enablement managers from multiple companies to ask their opinions on how to structure a sales enablement team. Despite all of them sharing their points of view based on vast experience, the answer from each was: 'It depends!' It depends on the budget, time-lines, skillsets, resources, tools, roles and responsibilities of different groups, senior management direction and even the maturity of the sales organization. Even after taking into consideration these factors, ongoing adjustments will have to be made based on a changing external environment as well as the fact that sales enablement itself is still evolving. Even though the end goal is the same, every company structures its sales enablement support based on what works, or what they believe will work for them at that time. Then, they are likely to pivot the team structure as time goes by.

Therefore, there's no standard method for developing a sales enablement team. My husband is an avid poker player, which is another arena in which you can't teach a single recipe for success. He was lucky enough to come across a short book early in his playing days, *Winning at Poker* by Jonathan Archer, in which the author doesn't attempt to go through all the different scenarios a player might encounter but instead explains appropriate thinking processes and strategies that can be adapted to many games and situations. Similarly, my goal is to explain how to analyse the sales team's needs and your available resources to structure the best possible team at a specific point in time.

You know that you will need to pivot, evaluate or re-evaluate the structure of a sales enablement team, when this happens:

8.1

- **tribal knowledge** is no longer scalable to support a growing sales team
- salespeople spend **too much time** creating and searching for content
- a lack of crisp product **positioning** is inhibiting successful sales conversions

- new hires are **not properly trained** and take too long to ramp against their quotas
- collaboration and communication suffer due to **organizational siloes**

It's about what you want to accomplish

While thinking through this chapter, I've come to the realization that I have asked the wrong question. It's not about 'how' to structure a team. The question I should have asked is 'what' do you want to accomplish with a sales enablement team? Figuring out the 'what' will guide you in choosing 'how' to build your team. Here is a process that you can use to define the 'what' and start putting together your team:

- understand business goals and the sales strategy
- comprehend the sales organization structure, methodologies and processes
- map the overall support structure of the sales team
- identify support gaps or more efficient ways to support the team
- define the sales enablement team's objectives and propose the team structure
- seek approval from management for a well thought-out plan
- put a team together and execute on the plan

Understand business goals and sales strategy

A team or a group should have a specific charter related to a company's business goals and objectives. If you want to create a team, you first need to tie your team's mission to your company's goals. After all, any group's contribution to a company should directly or indirectly support the overall business goals. For a sales enablement team, you not only need to articulate business goals, but also deeply understand how those relate to the overall sales strategy and the ability to achieve sales targets. Most companies' sales strategies will touch on the following:

- penetrate new target markets, geographies, verticals, or a combination
- launch new products or services
- identify how to upsell and cross-sell against an existing product portfolio
- limit customer churn and increase sales in existing markets or accounts
- improve customer support and services (not necessarily as post-customer support) to maintain customer relationships and drive better customer satisfaction

Defining your business goals and sales strategies will give you a context for discussing your proposed team structure with your senior management team in a way that makes benefits clear.

Comprehend the sales organization structure, methodology and processes

It's not enough to know just business goals and sales strategies. Throughout this book, I emphasize the importance of understanding sales methodologies and sales processes. The better you understand the sales team, the better you can design your sales enablement efforts to support them. Marketers create 'buyer personas' to personify their target audiences. They don't usually create a persona to support internal stakeholders. What about creating a sales persona to support the sales teams? Using this persona, you can articulate the typical day of a specific sales role including this person's role and responsibilities, experience, strengths, aspirations, challenges and pain points. You can even add common personality traits as part of the persona narrative. Solicit feedback from the sales team by focusing on overachievers and underachievers alike to get better insight.

The persona portrait will not only formalize your understanding of the different roles in the sales team, but also prioritize which sales roles you can best support as you get started. The sales personas can also be used for targeted recruiting and hiring. You may be asked to support all of them, but the prioritization recommendation by you will help drive conversations with sales management and will guide the structure of your sales enablement team.

Grasp the overall support structure of the sales team

Now that you know your sales team well and how sales enablement can be most effective, it's time to understand who is doing what to support the sales team. In general, almost every group inside a company supports sales, from human resources (HR), IT, accounting, finance, manufacturing, research and development to marketing. HR provide hiring, training, and performance management. IT provide tools and enabling technology support. Accounting may have a role in compensation and account billings. Finance is involved in forecasting, quota tracking, budget planning, pricing and margin as well as deal support. Manufacturing provides product available to promise (ATP), product forecast, etc. R&D helps prioritize and bring to market new offerings and capabilities to address market needs. You will need to understand how different functions are integrated with sales enablement and marketing to make sense of your team's role in the overall support structure.

Identify gaps or more efficient ways to support the sales team

The sales enablement function may have been created by a top-down driven initiative or could be the conglomeration of multiple functions from several different groups. Understanding how the current capabilities are arranged will help you gain a solid grasp on the sales enablement capabilities in your company.

Once you understand who is doing what, you can identify the gaps or recommend ideas to drive better efficiencies. It can also provide guidance for tweaking sales enablement's roles and responsibilities to minimize duplicate efforts. Gaining a clear view of how your team fits into the big intertwined corporate machine lets you define how you will work with other teams that support the sales group.

Define the sales enablement team's objectives and team structure

The next step after identifying the areas where you can provide value is to write the team objectives. What do you want the sales enablement team to accomplish? What are the desired outcomes and impacts? At this stage, you should have several objectives. Based on these objectives, you can create different options for the team structure. Remember, a team structure could include virtual components, or experts from other groups for some of the functions and even outsourced resources. Ultimately, whatever you suggest, you will need to get approval from the executive management. In my experience, it's beneficial to have several options encompassing the team's objectives and the team's structure when securing approval from executive management. Be ready to discuss the number of people you need and overall budget along with a clear timeline with key milestones. Your team structure is heavily dependent on the resources and budget you are able to secure from management.

Seek approval from management

When you discuss your proposal with management, you need to be able to articulate different options by highlighting each option's pros and cons as well as compromises being made. It is rare that marketing get everything they ask for and most management teams want to see that compromises have been made and carefully understood. Most importantly, you need to be able to explain the impact and your contribution to the sales team. Seek their approval on the team objectives and proposed team structure. This must include support for the sales team's management or this is likely to be an unwinnable uphill battle.

Put a team together

Whether you are leading a virtual team or a formal team, it's important to clearly identify objectives, goals and initiatives to provide a framework for the team members. In addition, you may need to hire new talent or shift team member roles. Once the team is in place (even if they are a partial team), have a kick-off meeting, share your plan and solicit feedback. Get everyone on the same page and make sure to address any concerns that may exist. You may not be able to get completely aligned in just one meeting, but it's important to start somewhere. I find that having a regular meeting (either weekly or bi-weekly) helps build the synergy of a team and keeps the momentum going. This is especially effective if you can have influencers from the sales team and key leaders.

Potential roles for a sales enablement team

Back-end support	Roles
Sales coaching and talent development	Sales coach or sales executive
Talent recruiting	Recruiter
Sales onboarding and training	Sales talent developer; training designer; training developer; training instructor/facilitator; sales research manager
Sales tools and process improvement	Sales operations manager; sales technology manager; IT manager; procurement manager
Sales incentives and compensation	Sales compensation manager; finance manager for sales; accounting manager for sales
Channel partner support	Channel partner sales enablement manager
Solutions and positioning	Messaging manager; marketing manager
Sales pipeline and forecast management	Sales executive; sales data analyst

Remember

Before putting a team together, here are steps you can take:

- understand business goals and sales strategies
- comprehend the sales organization structure, methodology and processes
- map the overall support structure of the sales team
- identify support gaps or more efficient ways to support the team
- define the sales enablement team's objectives and propose the team structures
- seek approval from management

Where should sales enablement reside?

I discussed the ownership of sales enablement in the Introduction to this book. The general verdict of over twenty sales enablement managers is that sales enablement should be part of the sale team and be a peer to sales operations, and not a part of sales operations. The reason is that sales operations tends to focus on deal support, quotas, pipeline, compensation, and processes with mostly short-term goals (month by month). Sales enablement's activities are related to training, content, hiring, lead generation and marketing collaboration. These processes have a longer cycle time and goals usually require multiple quarters to deliver full value. Therefore, it's important to separate sales enablement from sales operations. However, in some companies, they are merged into one group, which can create long-term vs. short-term conflicts that have to navigate through.

I have seen sales enablement reporting to marketing, sales, sales operations, finance, HR and even product teams. In some companies, sales enablement might be put under HR because one of the more important responsibilities of sales enablement is training, and HR is responsible for hiring and training company-wide. Amy Pence's training team at Alteryx was moved from sales to HR to scale her best practices across the corporation. In some companies, sales enablement is responsible for all sales dashboards and indicators, so logically they can report to finance. Chuck Steinhauser's team at Amdocs reported to sales operations before being moved to finance. Currently, they are evaluating a possible move back to the sales operations team.

In some cases, subject matter experts or product engineers are responsible for creating product training for the sales team and, therefore, sales enablement can be incorporated into the product teams. Emma Hitzke, Senior Marketing Manager for Intel's IoT division, leads the sales enablement team, who report to one of the product groups. Of course, since sales enablement are responsible for inside sales and lead generation, some companies place them under marketing. One example of this was at Limelight, where Michael King led the inside sales team as a marketing function. Again, there is no right or wrong answer to where sales enablement should reside and it can evolve over time. There are a variety of options, and each one comes with pros and cons. My recommendation is for sales enablement to stay with the sales team, but I completely understand that it's up to management to make that call.

> **Remember**
>
> When I talk to sales enablement managers, most still prefer to be part of the sales team and report directly to the vice president of sales. The sales team has better control over sales enablement priorities and are able to allocate budget and resources to support them. There is also the issue of ensuring that the sales team use the sales enablement tools. User adoption can be easier if salespeople are in charge of sales enablement and are on the hook for overall success.

When sales enablement report to other functions, there is always the risk of being deprioritized based on that group's focus, depriving sale enablement of required resources. The remedy is to request regular updates and agree on a service level agreement with success metrics.

Talent and skillsets

We all know that it's important to hire great people who are passionate, dedicated and fit into the company culture. But what qualities should a sales enablement person possess? This person is likely to act as a liaison between your sales, marketing, product teams and other internal stakeholders. Several sales enablement directors told me that they will only hire people who have been salespeople in the past. Sales reps can relate better to support team members who are intimately familiar with sales' pain points and challenges. It is a cliché but sales reps have more trust in other team members who have worked in a similar role in the past. Regardless, I have also discovered that it is important to command salespeople's respect, otherwise, they may challenge, stall or ignore your requests.

If you lead a virtual team, you may not have a lot of control over the team's make-up, so you may have to find ways to work with the resources available to you. If you do have the authority to hire full-time employees or contractors, you should refer to your objectives and use them as a compass to determine the mix of talent and skill-sets needed on your team.

Previously, I mentioned that there are common elements in various 'sales enablement' definitions:

- training
- coaching
- content
- cross-functional
- technology
- process – and of course
- people

Depending on your objectives and the initiatives you plan to implement, you may need to hire people able to cover those areas.

In general, these common skillsets are needed:

8.2

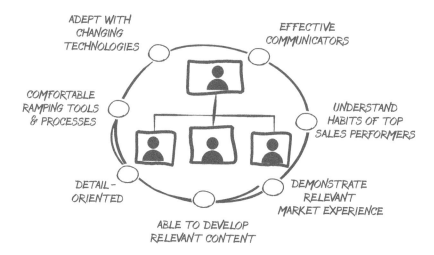

Ability to communicate effectively

Based on my conversations with sales enablement managers, this is probably the most important skill in the sales enablement job. Since sales enablement is a cross-functional role, team members will need to be comfortable talking to their sales teams, as well as teams from other departments and customers. After all, selling your solution can often require knowing details of various departments and functions including product, services, support and even engineering. Sales enablement need to be able to effectively communicate and navigate these departments to ensure the right knowledge is put in front of the sales reps in any given sales situation.

Part of communicating is listening. In order to better support your sales team, sales enablement also need to seek input and receive feedback from the sales team and other support groups.[1]

Understand the sales mentality of top performers

The mentality of a high-performing sales rep is different from that of most other employees. They are 'achievement-focused' and they certainly won't be easily discouraged. Understanding how they think and what they need will enable your team to help not only top performers, but also all salespeople. 'For example,' says JJ Fernoni, VP of sales at Guru, 'they don't want to waste time and they need to have immediate access to verified accurate, usable, consumable content so they can continue to advance sales cycles with minimal delays. Delays searching for information equals money lost.' The specific traits of top performers should also be included in the sales persona that I mentioned earlier.

Diane Walker, former Sales Enablement Manager for SAP, McAfee and HP, made sure that she stayed close to the top performers and understood their thinking processes and challenges. She did not tailor her support only to top performers, but she observed those top performers' challenges and applied those lessons to other team members. Understanding them helped her better support the sales team as a whole. By aligning with top performers, they can also be leveraged as advocates in front of other sales reps. Many reps want to emulate the top performers, and having their endorsement can be an important catalyst for your sales enablement programme.

Demonstrable relevant market experience

In general, sales enablement requires a team with members who have relevant experience that will be recognized by the other teams and especially sales reps. Relevant experience can be one or more of the following:

- **Industry experience:** Team members come from the industry your company is in and therefore have domain knowledge relevant to your business and target customers.
- **Sales experience:** Team members have sales or sales enablement experience gained from having worked for competitors or closely related companies, which provides the relevant credibility.
- **Product marketing experience:** Team members come from product or field marketing related roles and have experience developing contextual content relevant to your market and customers.

Ideally, the sales enablement team will have as many of the three attributes listed above as possible. This gives them more credibility as individuals, and more importantly in the relevancy of the work they generate.

Know how to create and find relevant content

Content is an interesting monster and a critical part of sales activities. According to a 2015 study, '57 percent of survey respondents cited high quality content as a topic driver of sales.'[2] Sales teams not only need content, but also need to be able to find the right content quickly. While 84 per cent of respondents indicated that content search and utilization was the number one area that could improve sales productivity, only 35 per cent of companies are actively working on this issue. And this understandably leads to wasted time. According to the study, 31 per cent of sales reps' time is spent searching for or creating content, and 20 per cent is spent on reporting, administrative and CRM-related tasks. Cisco is among the 35 per cent of companies working to make content easy to find. Ken Chizinsky, Senior Manager of User Experience (UX) for the Digital Sales Strategy and Design Team at Cisco, is fully aware of the issue. He and his team not only highlight the most popular content on SalesConnect, the content management library for their direct and indirect sales force, they also optimize their 'quick search' feature to help salespeople save time on content searches. Sourcing an appropriate tool or platform that the sales team can use to access content is an important element to help your sales team find the right content.

Thinking about *how* the content will be used by reps is the first step. It helps paint a clear picture for producing content efficiently. This comes from having the ability to tap into the sales mentality and understanding the problems they are trying to solve. 'Listen to sales pitches, calls, emails to see how and what is articulated to prospects' (Feroni again).

If your team is responsible for content creation, you need someone who can either write or produce content in different formats. Most importantly, they also need to know how to make content more consumable for their salespeople, especially top performers. Content creation is a collaboration between sales enablement, marketing and sometimes the product and R&D teams. Marketing is responsible for messaging, content and outbound communications. The sales enablement team can take what marketing creates and modify it to suit the sales team's needs by creating on-point and relevant content such as case studies, competitive information digests, proposal templates and prospect-facing informational material, as well as other collateral. To do so, they need to understand how to create different types of content that can be immediately used and put into action by the sales team. If content creation and customization are the responsibility of your sales enablement team, hiring talent with strong writing skills is vital. They will also need to have relevant industry or subject matter experience.

Attention to detail

Sales enablement is about paying attention to sales' needs. Similar to a concierge tending to guests' needs or an office manager facilitating smooth daily operations, you need to pay attention to details. Frequently, some of the details you notice are actually gaps that need to be served. Note your observations and propose a recommendation to solve them. Identifying the gaps doesn't mean that your team has to do all the work. Sometimes, that's the case. Sometimes, it's a collaborative effort with other groups. I understand that there may be inertia in a large organization that's hard to break through, but it's important to point out areas for continuous improvement and work to have them addressed.

Tenacity to ramp tools and processes

Ramping tools and process for the sales team can be difficult. We are all creatures of habit. Nobody likes to change, especially salespeople. They like to do things the same way and prefer the path of least resistance. They think that whatever they have been doing has worked so far, so why change? I find that ramping new tools and processes for the sales team is particularly challenging. You need to think creatively to get them to change and as much as possible demonstrate how the new capabilities will make it easier for them. Making the tools easy to use is a must. Creating incentives or financial awards helps too. Get buy-in from the VP of sales on tool implementation and make sure they stick past the initial rollout.

Typically, salespeople get paid for selling. Taking time to help implement or test new tools and processes is often perceived as time that could be better spent selling. In addition to showing them how the investment of their time will ultimately help them, you may need management help with some kind of compensation or quota relief. There's no doubt about it, ramping new tools and processes for the sales team is a challenging endeavour.

Comfortable working with ever-changing technologies

Business professionals requires a mental shift and the ability to get out of their comfort zone to adapt to the fast pace of technological change today. This is especially challenging for those who had years of work experience in an era when change had been slower. Scott Brinker, Program Chair at the Martech Conference, tries to make sense of the number of platforms and vendors that have launched every year since 2011. The marketing and sales technology landscape has grown from 150 vendors to over 5,000 solutions and vendors.

Having a firm grasp of the technologies used in both marketing and sales is challenging. Research, reading and self-learning will be part of our job scopes moving forward. We may have the same roles and responsibilities, but how the job will be done with technology's help requires us to learn and embrace new ways of working.

Supporting sales enablement across regions

Another key element that will impact a sales enablement team structure is the need to support sales teams in different countries. This tends to be a challenge for multinational companies such as IBM, Intel, Cisco, Coke, Toyota, etc and companies that are trying to expand globally. Again, there is no one-size-fits-all answer to achieving an effective support structure. It's a matter of collaboration between the headquarters and local teams and reaching agreement on who is doing what, who leads and who follows. That communication is vital for teams working in different time zones.

Remember

Here are some factors to take into account when creating a structure to support a global sales force:

- Align on sales enablement objectives and strategies with each region's or country's sales force.
- Understand the local team's needs, which could be unique to their culture or business practices.
- Define roles and responsibilities between the headquarters (HQ) and the local teams (geographies).
- Hold regular meetings to provide updates and foster two-way communication.
- Source tools that can scale to other countries and languages.

Keeping the communication channels open is key. Understand the local team's needs, discuss and define roles and responsibilities. The local teams want to get direction and guidance from the corporate team, but they are not necessarily fond of HQ telling them what to do. The HQ team need to find a balance between guiding and dictating. There are times when HQ need to put their foot down and insist that the local team follow certain processes, tools or dashboards to ensure consistency. Based on my years of working with local teams around the world, the local teams usually don't have issues following

HQ's guidance and direction. They only have issues when these rules and directions do not align with local strategies or put an undue burden on them, due to limited resources and budget. It's HQ's job to listen and understand. I have in the past made exceptions based on a local team's requests. To scale sales enablement efforts across regions is a matter of give and take between HQ and geographies.

Sales teams in each region or territory tend to care about the accounts in their region or country, unless the account is global with a cross-regional presence. In general, global accounts are likely to be multinational companies that are managed directly from HQ. In those cases, the HQ sales team is likely to assign or hire salespeople on the ground, so they have a local presence to support those customers. The overall sales strategy for these accounts is very much driven by corporate HQ with local feedback. The local teams focus on providing the best support possible.

'Glocal' sales content requires special attention

Global sales content support is tricky, especially customization and localization. Some content can be scaled as is, some may need to be 'glocalized', which means translated or customized to meet local needs. Sarah Mitchell, Content Strategist at Lush Media and a localization expert, calls attention to key elements to consider for localization:

8.3

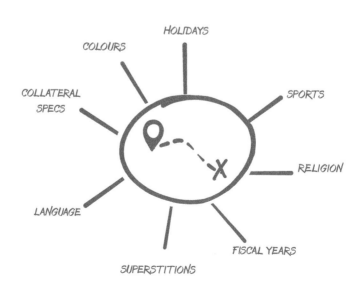

COLOURS HOLIDAYS SPORTS RELIGION FISCAL YEARS SUPERSTITIONS LANGUAGE COLLATERAL SPECS

- **Colours:** The colour of a wedding dress is not white in some countries.

- **Holidays:** Chinese New Year, Jewish New Year, Islamic New Year.

- **Sports:** Football in the US vs football in the rest of the world.

- **Religion:** Beliefs and rules.

- **Fiscal years:** In China one of the biggest shopping days is 11 November (Singles Day), which is equivalent to the US Black Friday after Thanksgiving.

- **Superstitions:** In Chinese the word for 'four' sounds like the word for 'death'. In some buildings, floor numbering goes straight from three to five.

- **Language usage:** Quid = buck = loonie = dosh = money. Not to mention analyse vs analyze, theatre vs theater. Litres vs gallons. Technical and medical terminology.

- **Collateral specifications:** Letter vs A4.

> **Remember**
>
> Be cognizant of word usage. Make sure that the local teams review translated content with appropriate localization and customization.

Creative localization

The headquarters team may decide the overall creative direction for a worldwide campaign. However, not all creative works in every region. A popular Old Spice campaign is so US-specific that its creative approach won't work for other countries. Check out the YouTube video 'Old Spice – the man your man could smell like'.[3] Yet, as the YouTube video 'Apple "global" ad in different countries' shows, the Apple iPhone creative approach can easily scale to different languages.[4]

The creative approach for print formats such as product briefs, white papers or other written content content is easier to scale. It will be more challenging for video production or even VR/AR/MR sales demos. HQ and local teams need to have a conversation about the creative angle ahead of content production.

> **Remember**
>
> For the creative approach, HQ take the lead and local teams need to review the creative and provide feedback. HQ need to understand that some creative may not work in some countries and you need to find a compromise.

Messaging localization

The product messaging and value proposition depends on product customizations and each region's target audience. Headquarters can create the messaging framework, but they can't force it on the local team. A couple of years ago, my marketing team decided to highlight the data security feature for our upcoming product launch. However, my team in China made it very clear to me that they can't use 'data security', since the Chinese government is very sensitive about the word 'security'. Instead, we agreed to go with 'reliability' as a key message for the Chinese product launch.

> **Remember**
>
> The messaging framework is usually led by HQ. If the products are tailored to local customers, product messaging and value propositions may need to be done by the local teams. Have an open discussion about value propositions, messaging framework and key sales talking points to ensure communications consistency.

Campaign theme/tagline localization

In some companies, campaigns are closely tied to sales offerings and efforts. Campaign themes and taglines, in most cases, need to be localized. Based on my experience working with local teams, I don't ask them to directly translate the theme or tagline. I make sure they understand the key insights and essence, then trust that they will customize it by using the proper text to bring the core messages to life.

Remember

It's the job of HQ to help local teams understand the campaign theme and tagline selection. The local team need to make their best effort to stay with the spirit of the theme and tagline selection, as well as follow the brand guide.

Content localization

The local team should have ownership of what to translate and customize for sales content. With limited budget and resources, the local team won't be able to translate everything. The HQ team need to plan their content roadmap in advance so that local teams know what's coming and can prioritize. This will allow them to think about how the local sales team will use the content, what the campaign will look like and where the content will be syndicated. Understanding the campaign and syndication channels will help them determine the needed formats of different content pieces.

It's important to map out campaigns before content is created and work with the local teams so they are fully engaged. I know this is very challenging, since they are in execution mode all the time. However, a general idea on how a campaign will run helps the HQ team determine the format requirements during the planning stage.

Globalization is complicated. How to strike that balance between global and local is really both an art and a science. It requires planning, collaboration, budget and resources.

Cross-region sales enablement

Iris Chan, CMO for Fusion Grove, was previously IBM's and Cisco's Sales and Marketing Manager for the Asia Pacific region. As a regional person working closely with headquarters, she experienced first-hand the support from corporate marketing and sales. She has worked closely with the corporate team on content localization for both sales and marketing efforts. In general, the lead generation effort was the regional managers' job with minimal help from the corporate office. She understood that it's challenging for marketing managers to support several regions and many countries from the corporate office. However, it is important to solicit local feedback, especially in tools, processes and content creation.

Here are some of the challenges she consistently encountered over the years with multiple companies:

- top-down driven approach without a full understanding of local challenges
- sales and marketing content are not tailored to local needs
- lack of local budget and resource support
- the delicate balance of global vs local
- no formal feedback loop from local to corporate to address local needs

Her recommendations for marketers who are also responsible for supporting sales in other regions and countries:

- gather feedback from local teams
- plan with a bottom-up mindset
- involve local teams as early as possible during the value proposition and content creation stage

Even if you can't do anything, sometimes it's just good to 'listen'. Her recommendations echo the steps that I outlined for different localization and customization of content collaborations. It's about listening, soliciting feedback and being open-minded. After all, the corporate and local offices are all part of the same team.

Remember

Communication. Compromise. Collaboration. While working through the cross-regional sales enablement support structure, you need to solicit and listen to the local teams' feedback. Sometimes, the HQ team will lead. Sometimes, the local teams will take the initiative. Keep the communications channel open and be open-minded.

The sales enablement team structure is fluid

Sales enablement is necessary, especially for complex selling. But in order to do a good job enabling sales, you need to decide what the team want to accomplish, where the team should reside, and how the team should be organized. The organizational structure of the sales team will change as the company grows or merges, and so will the sales enablement team structure. Sales training and development should not be the only thing that sales enablement do. Team members need to proactively understand sales' challenges and identify areas that can use additional help. Of course, in a big company you need to be careful not to step on other groups' toes. However, I have found that there are always some gaps that no one is working on. It's a matter of diagnosing and finding the challenges and working with the relevant stakeholders to prioritize and address them. You don't necessarily own fixing the issue, but if it's not yours to address, you should find the right person or team to deal with it. You are still adding value.

Sometimes you may have no control over the organizational structure or do not have the right talent to support your mission. It's all part of the journey. Do what you can with what you have and where you are.

What you can do

1 Assess the current stage of your sales enablement support structure.

2 If you are the sales enablement lead, craft the sales enablement objectives and document the required team structure.

3 Identify the talent and skillsets needed for your team.

Notes

1 JJ Feroni. 5 skills every sales enablement hire must have. Guru, 27 January 2016. https://blog.getguru.com/5-skills-every-sales-enablement-hire-must-have

2 Emma Brudner. Salespeople only spent one-third of their time selling last year. Hubspot, 31 August 2017. https://blog.hubspot.com/sales/salespeople-only-spent-one-third-of-their-time-selling-last-year

3 Old Spice – the man your man could smell like. www.youtube.com/watch?v=owGykVbfgUE

4 Jonathon Wilson. Apple 'global' ad in different countries. www.youtube.com/watch?v=MoE9XxXUatA&feature=youtu.be

It's complicated 09

The blessings and curses of technology

The great growling engine of change – technology.
ALVIN TOFFLER

I often say that technology is both a blessing and a curse. It makes our jobs easier and harder at the same time. Technology makes it easy to create new technologies. The commoditization of technology is democratizing the sales and marketing stack, levelling the playing field by removing barriers to entry. As technology continues to decline in price, we can afford to add numerous applications to our sales and marketing tech stack. But, if you are not careful about managing your sales and marketing tech stacks, you can end up using numerous applications, some of which can impede sales and marketing productiveness and efficiency. And that's where the curse comes from.

I ran into the mother of one of my son's classmates from back in elementary school while shopping recently. As mothers, we immediately started filling each other in about how the kids are doing. She told me that her son did something special during the summer. He researched online, bought all the components and assembled a desktop computer by himself. Do kids do that nowadays? In my experience, that's extremely rare. Children these days are excellent *consumers* of technology, but rarely dig into the bones of how it all works. I feel that's how we, as business professionals, have become. Technology has made it so easy for us that we don't spend time to understand how everything ties together and what we can do to improve.

Technology is driving social change the likes of which occurs only every few hundred years. The Pax Romana (Roman peace) of the Roman Empire, the Islamic Golden Age led by the Abbasids, the Tang Dynasty of China and the Industrial Revolution in Britain have led to today's information-based digital transformation. I don't know what

future generations will call the age marked by the end of the twentieth century and the beginning of the twenty-first, but I wouldn't be
surprised if it's something like the 'Information Renaissance', 'Pre-AI
Stone Age' or even the 'Pre-Skynet' era[1] (from the *Terminator* movies,
for those pessimists amongst us). Whatever it may be, I am grateful
to live in the twenty-first century to witness the information renaissance, yet I am deeply overwhelmed trying to make total sense of
it. I am still in awe when I think that Google is only 20 years old
(founded in 1998), Facebook only 14 (2004) and the iPhone only
11 (2007). Yet we use them as if they've been there our whole lives,
which for young adults is completely true. My boys have no memory
of what lives were like pre-Google, Facebook and iPhone. Frankly,
I have no memory of pre-Google, Facebook and iPhone, either. My
husband remembers a time in the 1980s when, as a field service tech,
he had a box full of maps in his car in order to be able to find his
assignments. Now, just one of many apps on his phone takes care of
that. Technology certainly has altered our behaviour and lifestyle. It
has changed how we, as marketers, reach our target customers. For
sales reps, it has added not only new venues to engage and research
but also new approaches to sell, so that we need to constantly learn
and adapt. Most importantly, technology has given power to buyers
to self-educate, find feasible solutions and contact salespeople on
their own terms.

The flipside of self-empowered buyers is that they are actively
searching, consuming, sharing and commenting on content online,
which leave traces and digital footprints that savvy analysts can
exploit. But the amount of data created by buyers is so overwhelming that marketers and salespeople are struggling to analyse it in
order to gain actionable insights. I discussed the complexity of the
marketing tech stack as many enterprises, private companies and
start-ups build different products and platforms to serve known and
unknown marketing and sales needs. Scott Brinker's Martech 5000
displays it all. For 2017 he captured 4,891 companies with 5,381
solutions in six categories: advertising and promotion, content and
experience, social and relationships, commerce and sales, data, and
management.[2] It's just mind-bogglingly overwhelming (and too big
to reproduce in this book).

Although Brinker's big map is more marketing-focused, Nicolas de Kouchkovsky, founder of CaCube Consulting, published Sales Tech Landscape 2017, which concentrated on the sales-centred tech stack. Sales technologies and platforms are another area that is reminiscent of the Wild West. De Kouchkovsky identified over 700 vendors in five sales-focused categories: engagement, productivity and enablement, sales intelligence, pipeline and analytics, and people management.[3]

He did a good job further dividing vendors from those big five categories into thirty-two sub-categories from email tools, content enablement, database and list services, price optimization, territory and quote management, incentives and commissions down to onboarding and training. The way he structured the platform and technologies is great and I don't get overwhelmed when I look at the overall graph. I can also use this infographic to help with pointers when I'm trying to find solutions and don't know where to start.

With so many players in the field, everyone is vying for buyers' attention. Therefore, the cost of acquiring customers continues to increase at a faster and faster pace. In addition, sales and marketing not only need to promote their unique value propositions, but they also need to spend time and effort to educate potential customers about the benefits of their offerings and to onboard, or familiarise, new customers. All these efforts cost money. Yet, the purchasing cycle is getting longer, which impacts cash flow. I use myself as an example: it took over a year from the time I became aware of Buffer until I finally purchased a subscription for the social media post and management service. And the purchase cycle is even longer for enterprises and complex technology sales. To increase revenue, the pure subscription model is no long sufficient for SaaS-based companies. Many also layer services on top of the platform to increase their revenue.

It's hard to predict the future. One school of thought is that the number of applications and services in the sales technology stack will continue to grow as new technologies such as xR, 3D printing and advanced analytics continue to emerge. Another school of thought predicts a series of consolidations and closures as the cost of updating software to remain competitive and customer acquisition continues to grow. A CEO of an SaaS-based platform company told me that

50 per cent of his revenue goes back into acquiring new customers. Maintaining and controlling acquisition cost will be a key challenge for SaaS-based or complex technology sales companies.

Set aside predictions about the future of the marketing and sales tech stack and let's ask ourselves about the real purpose of technology. Pawan Deshpande, CEO of Curata, said it succinctly: 'The function of technology is to help us to do things better, faster and cheaper.' It's true! Better, faster and cheaper is about automation, efficiency, and productivity. When I had a conversation with Peter Sandeen, messaging and position consultant, he summarized the purpose of technology similarly, but expanded a bit. He said technology has two functions – it enables us to:

- automate our existing processes
- enable new usage to do things we could not do before

The categories make a lot of sense to me. However, it's getting harder and harder to draw the boundary between automation and new usage, because companies continue to improve their tools with new features. For example: the initial CRM system was a tool to capture all customer contacts and engagement records, thereby automating a specific part of sales engagement. As CRM has evolved, more features have been added, such as dashboards, pipeline tracking, mobile app access, and even embedded analytics to predict customers' propensity to buy. These additional features morph CRM from pure automation to a platform that enables sales to do things they could not do before. Modern CRM serves automation and new usage.

Another example is Uber. Although Uber is revolutionary, strictly speaking it's just another form of taxi service. It enables us to hail a cab from wherever we are in a way that we could not before. In that way, Uber both automates and adds new features that didn't previously exist. It also applies a model of employment to the livery service industry in a way that hasn't been done before, through the use of new and existing tools (Uber driver's app and global positioning system (GPS) apps like Google Maps). It helps us do things better, faster and cheaper.

As sales and marketing professionals, we can source and leverage a relevant mix of the sales and marketing stack to make us productive and efficient. The biggest hidden competitive advantage lies in insights drawn by in-depth analytics through the combination of big data analytics and artificial intelligence. Big data analytics and artificial intelligence both require a massive amount of data to start. Big data analytics is the process of examining large and varied data sets to uncover hidden patterns, unknown correlations, market trends, customer preferences and other useful information that can help organizations make more-informed business decisions. It's about finding previously unseen insights to help us make better decisions. AI is defined as intelligence exhibited by machines.[4] Big data analytics shows us what has happened by identifying trends and patterns, which is defined as 'descriptive analytics'. Businesses can take one step further by using the identified patterns and trends to predict what could happen in the future based on previous trends and patterns,[5] which is called 'predictive analytics'. Again, you can take one step further by simulating the future under various sets of assumptions and scenarios to answer the question: 'What should business do?' That is described as 'prescriptive analytics'. Businesses will write their own proprietary code to build their own models, purchase third-party software or use both options to conduct these analyses. Many third-party analytic tools embed AI-based algorithm to aid the analysis. One of the most notable examples for sales is AI for CRM, Salesforce Einstein, from Salesforce.com.

Remember

Using a proper set of applications and tools will make sales and marketing more productive. The biggest hidden competitive advantage lies in insights drawn by analytics through the combination of big data analytics and artificial intelligence.

Three types of analytics:

- Descriptive: What has happened based on past trends and patterns?
- Predictive: What could happen in the future based on past trends and patterns?
- Prescriptive: What should business do?

To share technology's role in sales enablement, I will cover this topic with a focus on three key aspects:

- selecting a mix of sales stack and martech tools for different stages of the sales process
- identifying customer insights through descriptive and predictive analytics
- discovering relevant customers and predicting their next moves via artificial intelligence

Select tools at different stages of the sales process

I discussed the steps of sourcing sales enablement tools earlier. However, if you are evaluating and sourcing tools for the whole sales organization, the steps are slightly different. The key difference is to make sure that you have a holistic sales stack overview. In addition, sales enablement sourcing is more about the sales enablement team's needs. Sourcing the sales tech stack is about the whole sales organization, possibly including support groups. You need to understand the existing applications that the sales team are using. You also need to anticipate what the sales team want to accomplish in the next two or three years. It's about knowing what they need and don't need. Mark Godley, President of Lead Genius, suggested that it's critical to look at the sales and marketing stack together and emphasized the importance of asking the right questions:[6]

- Does everything in the sales stack solve a business problem?
- Are we using vanity metrics (likes, leads and engagement) and overlooking the analytics we need to understand our business (eg client acquisition costs and lifetime value of a customer)?
- Is the tech stack serving marketing and sales needs while delivering targeted information at the right time to buyers?

- What are our strategic objectives for the design and development of our sales and marketing stacks? What do we need to do that job?

- Are we taking the time to understand the landscape of available data solutions? Do we even know the essential data elements that will give us the biggest bang for the buck? Is it intent data? Technographics? Company firmographics? And who are the two or three data vendors that will deliver 80 per cent of the value to our business?

- As we begin to layer the necessary data sets, how do we cobble together a coherent, well-managed strategy? How do we integrate disparate data and resolve conflicting data to create actionable information for our salespeople?

- Do we need help with the difficult task of managing a stack built on multiple third-party data vendors and first-party data?

- Are we putting quality and results above quantity?

Helpful hints

Selecting the right tools requires you to ask the right questions:

- What business problems do we want to solve?
- How do we measure the success of specific tools?
- How does the tool help our customers?
- How does the tool fit into the overall sales and marketing tech stacks?
- How do we balance quality vs quantity if the tool aims to drive volume?

These are not easy questions to answer, yet asking questions forces you and the team to work to truly understand your own tech stack's needs. Treat this process as necessary soul-searching.

Starting with the questions above, you can take the following steps to source your tech stack. Depending on how sourcing is done within your company and the sales team, modify the steps as you see fit:

- Document the questions: Work with the team to answer the questions. These questions will guide the direction of sourcing your tech stack.

- Anticipate the needs of the sales team: Observe and interview the sales team. Ask them to articulate as much as they can about current and future needs and challenges. If you have a persona profile for your sales team, it will come in handy at this stage.

- Map existing tools to the sales process: Understand the sales processes and existing sales technology stack and identify how the sales tech stack integrates into the overall sales process.

- Comprehend the gaps in existing tools: Compare sales needs from bullet point one to the existing tools' capabilities. Document pros and cons of existing tools and identify the gaps.

- Propose the technical requirements to address the gap analysis: Based on the gap analysis, you can identify specific technical requirements that you need to close the gaps.

- Research potential tools that meet the requirements: Conduct research, talk to vendors, watch demos and test free trials. Nicolas's sales stack landscape can come in handy.

- Form a sourcing team: Determine the right people who need to be involved in making sourcing decisions, including procurement, IT and other groups. Build alignment among internal stakeholders. Depending on the scope, the decision can be made by sales executives.

- Evaluate the recommendations: Narrow down vendor selections and further evaluate the product features and compare with needs.

- Make a decision: The team makes a decision based on selection criterial and senior management buy-in.

The process sounds linear, but it's usually one-step forward and two-steps backward, especially in a large enterprise. In addition, it can be challenging to have a full picture of the sales process and all the sales tools in a big enterprise. The key is to do the best you can to gather as much information as you need. Sometimes, you'll feel like a blind person touching an elephant. I have found that your understanding will shape what tools you'll need to source. It's better to be patient and spend time up-front to understand sales needs, sales processes, methodology and existing tools. The information is out there, it's a matter of spending time to piece the puzzle together.

Selecting new tools for your sales stack is important. Sometimes, your evaluation might lead to the conclusion that you should terminate the use of some tools or consolidate multiple tools into a single one used across the organization. According to the 2017 Martech Industry Council research results, the average stack includes sixteen technologies, 25 per cent have twenty or more tools, and a few have close to a hundred technologies. When asked about their greatest frustration, it's not surprising that half admit they have too many technologies and 49 per cent complain about poor integration.[7] You will need to address the balance of productivity, quality of leads and number of applications to determine if your technology is getting in the way of desired results. Mark Godley told me that they took a 'less is more' approach in 2017 and pruned their stack by about a dozen vendors. They are more focused, working more efficiently and closing more business as a result of that action. It's critical to take a step back and understand why you use specific technology.

Another caveat to bear in mind: technology will not solve your problems if the underlying data quality has issues or inconsistencies. Data cleaning is a critical element of data analytics that is often overlooked by management. Before embarking on a completely new technology stack, it's important to make sure that data is clean and get agreement from all the departments that will use the data on clear definitions of critical data elements. For example, a contact has certain attributes that inside sales care about, other attributes that are important to outside sales and yet additional attributes that operations and accounting need. Getting clarity and agreement on data definitions can yield great benefits even without a technology adjustment.

ROI never comes just from installing the software du jour or having a 'complete' tech stack. ROI comes from having a solid strategy, tight integration and streamlined processes. Some companies will position their tools and technology as an end-to-end solution. The reality is that no vendor's solution is a panacea to solve world hunger and address every sales challenge. You will use different tools for different stages of sales processes. The key thing is integration and making the trade-off between tools. Processes and tools need to be closely tied together.

> **Remember**
>
> Identifying the needs of a sales tech stack is a soul-searching process. The following steps can help you source the right tools:
>
> - document your needs and challenges
> - map existing tools to the sales process
> - comprehend the gaps in existing tools
> - propose the technical requirements to address the gap analysis
> - research potential tools that meet the requirements
> - form a sourcing team
> - evaluate the recommendations
> - make a decision

Creating customers insights through descriptive and predictive analytics

In the digital era, almost everything we do online is traceable or trackable. Your clicks on likes or shares, your search using voice and keyboards, your downloads of content are clues and signals for salespeople and marketers. Based on our behaviour, sales and marketing people will make a 'best guess' about our 'intent' and what our next move might be. With that guesstimation, marketers will make an effort to serve relevant content or implement personalized or retargeted outreach to facilitate customers' move to the next stage of the purchase cycle.

In addition, we, as consumers and business professionals, generate a huge amount of structured and unstructured data every day. We text our friends and family, share photos on social media, upload presentations on SharePoint or Dropbox, exchange emails, download music and more. Every time we touch our computers, tablets and smartphones we are generating data and the movements are captured somewhere. According to Domo's fifth annual infographic, 'How much data is generated every minute?', 90 per cent of all data today was created in the past two years which is 2.5 quintillion bytes of data per day. As a whole, the internet population has grown by 7.5 per cent since 2016 with a total of over 3.7 billion people. We send 3.5 million text messages per minute. Among the activities that contribute to this exponential increase in data are such items as: 'Uber taking 45,787 trips each minute, Spotify adding 13 new songs, we tweet 456,000 times, post 46,740 Instagram photos, Google 3.6 million searches, and publish 600 new page edits on Wikipedia each minute. The Internet also copes with 103,447,520 spam emails every minute.'[8] With so much data, there are bound to be some insights that we can discover to validate our hypotheses, help us better optimize our sales and marketing outreach, and better understand our customers.

Here is a great example of using big data analytics to correlate information from various sources to find high-quality leads. In 2017, Curata wanted to identify target accounts that the sales teams could go after by using an account-based approach for a new product called Curata Content Marketing Platform. Their product integrates with Marketo, Eloqua or Pardot among other systems to measure the performance of content marketing. Based on their understanding of their ideal customer profile (ICP), and years of interactions with their customers, they concluded that companies who use Marketo, Eloqua or Pardot to create large volumes of marketing content on a regular basis would be highly interested in their product. To find companies that fit these criteria, they first wanted to find out which companies use Marketo, Eloqua and Pardot. Their CEO, Pawan Deshpande, and the engineering team wrote an application that would crawl and analyse the marketing automation systems used on over 200,000 company websites. From that analysis, they constructed a long list of companies. Then, they narrowed down that list by analysing the blogs and content resource pages on these companies' websites to gauge the size of their content marketing efforts. The companies with lots of content tended to have a higher propensity to use Curata tools. Therefore, they further narrowed down the list with that criterion. With that revised list, they cross-referenced over 100,000 leads in their CRM database and LinkedIn to identify potential prospects with digital marketing or content related titles. They ran a descriptive analysis to gauge 'What is the level of content marketing efforts on these websites?' They then conducted predictive analysis to determine 'What are the list of companies and contacts that they reach out to based on correlations with their existing database?' After analysing your company's ICP, you may be able to leverage similar analyses to create a list of high-quality leads.

Once Curata had their filtered results, marketing came in and ran targeted accounted-based marketing. The marketing team ran integrated campaigns using AdWords Customer Match, Twitter, Facebook ads, and customized email outreach. Based on the content consumed by their campaigns, Curata marketing scored and prioritized these accounts' interest in engaging with the sales team. That priority list became the sales team's high-quality lead list. The sales team would go through the list and cherry-pick the top 30 accounts that they wanted to target. Working with marketing, the company would send these prospects goodie boxes. The sales team used the goodie box as a conversation starter to engage with prospects.

They made certain hypotheses on the types of customers that they believed would have a high probability of conversion. Then, they conducted in-depth analysis and correlated with different data sources to identify targeted accounts before doing any top-of-funnel marketing. It reversed the traditional marketing approach of building mass top-of-the-funnel awareness. It does not mean that brand awareness is not important for Curata. Pawan and his marketing team still sponsors select events and leverage content marketing to drive inbound traffic. This is a fantastic example of account-based marketing made smarter with big data analytics.

Remember

An approach to big data analytics:

- Articulate the specific problem that you want to solve.
- Understand the impact if this problem is solved.
- Create propensity-to-buy hypotheses based on your understanding of how your customers behave or act. If they do this or have that attribute, then they are likely to buy.

- Identify the relevant data sources to conduct analysis.
- Build a model and conduct analysis by writing your own code, hiring an analytics firm or using third-party tools.
- Cross-correlate with other external sources, if necessary.
- Review the results.
- Optimize and modify the model and analysis.
- Agree on the results by relevant stakeholders.
- Implement the findings.

Discovering relevant customers and predicting their moves via AI

AI is already part of our lives, even if it's not overtly apparent. Google harnesses AI to autocomplete search queries, predicting what you are searching for with great accuracy. Facebook news feeds and Amazon product recommendations are tailored to your preferences based on your content consumption and product purchases. Spotify, Pandora and Apple Music all have certain machine-learning algorithms built into their applications to make decisions about which new songs or artists to recommend by associating listeners' preferences with attributes of songs in their database. Alexa and Google Home have already become the new normal for many households. These 'intelligent' gadgets are able to recognize speech, analyse the information they have access to, and provide logical, appropriate and intelligent answers or solutions (sometimes).

The goal of AI is to create intelligent machines that work and react like humans. In order for machine to 'think' or 'act' like humans, we need to teach them how to learn. For machines to learn, it's best to feed them massive amounts of data and build algorithms for computers to begin teaching themselves. Machine learning means 'Algorithms that parse data, learn from that data, and then apply what they've learned to make informed decisions.'[9] Machine learning fuels all sorts of automated tasks across multiple industries, from data security firms hunting down malware to finance professionals setting parameters for favourable trades. Well-known examples of machines learning are product recommendations and movie suggestions from Amazon and Netflix.[10]

Another common term used in AI is 'deep learning', which is a subset of machine learning. As defined by Brett Grossfeld, 'A deep learning model is designed to continually analyze data with a logic structure similar to how a human would draw conclusions. To achieve this, deep learning uses a layered structure of algorithms called an artificial neural network (ANN). The design of an ANN is inspired by the biological neural network of the human brain. This makes for machine intelligence that's far more capable than that of standard machine learning models.'[11] The tricky part is that a deep learning model doesn't always draw correct conclusions, so results need to be evaluated or you run the risk of basing decisions and future work on faulty premises. But when it works, functional deep learning is a scientific marvel and the potential backbone of true artificial intelligence.

So, what does AI, machine learning and deep learning mean to sales and marketing? Consumer apps have trained consumers to expect more from businesses. They expect businesses to deliver a seamless experience and anticipate their needs without being creepy and intrusive. As part of lead analysis, AI is a powerful tool to provide accurate lead scoring and weighting. This helps increase the probability of identifying high-quality target customers who are interested in learning more and moving to the next stage of the purchase cycle. AI can also assist in presenting dynamic content and personalized product offerings to the right customers at the right time. It applies throughout the sales process and purchase journey wherever automation or analytics can be done.

Companies find leads using different approaches. Some focus on gathering leads via trade shows. Others use various online outbound marketing tactics to entice potential customers to their companies' website and contact form pages. Some work closely with demand generation companies. Sanjit Singh, Chief Operation Officer at LeadCrunch, a predictive marketing company, explained how they use AI to discover high-quality leads for Odyssey Logistics & Technology Corporation (Odyssey).[12] This logistics company has been using traditional methods such as attending tradeshows and purchasing cold call lists to generate leads that were inefficient, cumbersome and slow. They decided to try a different approach by working with a predictive marketing company with demand generation campaign capabilities. LeadCrunch proposed specific steps to work with Odyssey:

- Build an audience of prospects similar to Odyssey's top customers.
- Engage relevant contacts at these target companies with thought leadership content through strategic touchpoints.
- Validate engagement.
- Further nurture leads with additional content.
- Share content engagement data with Odyssey.
- Assess the level of buyers' interest by having the Odyssey sales team reach out to book demos.

These steps are similar to components of a typical content-marketing based lead generation approach. Many companies do that. The key difference is how LeadCrunch curates target companies. Singh explained that the company asked Odyssey to provide the names of its top twenty-five business customers. LeadCrunch then fed the data into its AI-based predictive targeting system, DeepFind. This tool analysed millions of data points across the digital footprints of Odyssey's best customers and produced Odyssey's best customer 'DNA blueprint'. LeadCrunch then used that blueprint to find look-alike prospects. To further gauge the prospects' intent and interest, LeadCrunch used various marketing outreach techniques to share Odyssey content. LeadCrunch then established interest in the content and nurtured the leads with additional content. Odyssey's sales team then reached out to book demos with prospects armed with insights from the content engagement data and other data points. With the targeted look-alike customer approach, the quality of leads was substantially better than that of trade shows and traditional list and data providers. As a result of creating a look-alike prospect list, Odyssey was able to boost its pipeline by 34 per cent. This look-alike approach is similar to the way that online advertising companies such as Facebook and Google create look-alike audiences.

While Odyssey's challenge was trying to find new leads, the challenge for CenturyLink, one of the largest telecommunications providers in the United States, was not the volume of the leads, but the need to find a cost-effective way to comb through thousands of leads to identify high-quality leads without hiring an army of inside salespeople. The company approached this issue by using an AI-powered sales assistant made by Conversica to see if it could help the company identify hot leads by analysing and evaluating its database. The Conversica AI, a virtual assistant named Angie, sends about 30,000 emails a month and interprets the responses to determine potential hot leads. Angie, powered by AI through machine learning, could understand 99 per cent of the emails she received; the 1 per cent that she couldn't understand were sent to her manager. Angie routes the right leads to the right reps. She even sets appointments for the appropriate salesperson and seamlessly hands off the conversation to that human.

'According to Scott Berns, CenturyLink's Director of Marketing Operations, the company has approximately 1,600 salespeople, and the Angie pilot started with four of them. That number soon rose to 20 and continues to grow today. Initially, Angie was identifying about 25 hot leads per week. That has now increased to 40, and the results have certainly validated the company's investment. It has earned $20 in new contracts for every dollar it spent on the system.'[13]

Tom Wentworth, Chief Marketing Officer at RapidMiner, a company that provides an analytical tool for data scientists, had a similar problem managing lead volume. Like many software companies, RapidMiner offers free trials but was struggling to serve the high volume of users that took advantage of the offer. In addition, many RapidMiner users also need assistance to get the most out of the trial. The salespeople were overwhelmed, and were spending a great deal of time sorting through the chat sessions to find potential customers.

Wentworth implemented DriftBot, which uses an intelligent chatbot to qualify and book meetings for the sales team. Rather than focusing on filling out the contact form and following up with email, this tool focuses on having human-like conversational chats with prospects who come to their website. Wentworth set up the workflow and mapped out possible communications scenarios. DriftBot now conducts about a thousand chats per month, resolving about two-thirds of the customer inquiries. It routes those that it cannot resolve to human salespeople. In addition to Wentworth, who is monitoring the tool's interactions, two co-op college students support the inquiries part-time. Wentworth stated that Drift is generating qualified leads for the sales team. 'It's the most productive thing I'm doing in marketing,' he said.

Wentworth reviews daily conversations people have had with DriftBot. 'I've learned things about my visitors that no other analytics system would show,' said Wentworth. 'We've learned about new use cases, and we've learned about product problems.'

Remember

Both Conversica and Drift offer AI sales assistants in different ways, but both tools try to emulate human thinking processes and to respond like a human being. These AI-based agents are not necessarily replacing sales and marketing people. They automate and zip through the lead qualification process in a faster and more efficient way, so salespeople don't waste time on low quality leads.

This is one of the biggest strengths of an AI agent that can elicit information like a person, rather than an analytics tool that simply finds patterns in the data it collects. It also allows for specific steps to be addressed before a human takes over to either complete sales or address customers' issues. Using an AI agent also requires marketing to create a playbook complete with messaging, targeting, workflow and content, which is the essence of sales enablement. When it comes to AI in business, it's about using AI to help customers address their immediate needs. It's about scaling helpfulness. Hopefully, by doing so, marketing and inside sales can identify higher qualified leads faster and cheaper.

Humans vs human-like machines

In 1956, John McCarthy, a computer science professor at Stanford, coined the term artificial intelligence,[14] which described a world in which machines could 'solve the kinds of problems now reserved for humans'. AI continues to evolve and branch out in several directions. Most of the mainstream AI-based tools have turned toward domain-dependent and problem-specific solutions. They are designed to perform specific tasks to accomplish short-term goals. Alexa and Google Home respond to our questions and solve our short-term needs. Sales assistants from Conversica and Drift address customers' immediate needs and focus on specific tasks. Although they are getting better and better at emulating human-like responses, these AI-based tools are still oriented around specific tasks, which is referred to as weak AI or narrow AI.

In January 2015 an open letter on AI was signed by such luminaries as Stephen Hawking and Elon Musk. While acknowledging AI's benefits and potentials, it cautioned against potential dire consequences. Hawking told the BBC: 'The primitive forms of artificial intelligence we already have have proved very useful. But I think the development of full artificial intelligence could spell the end of the human race.'[15] Technology entrepreneur Elon Musk has also described the rise of AI as 'our biggest existential threat.' The specific AI field that Hawking and Musk referred to is artificial general intelligence (AGI), strong AI or human-like AI, and artificial super intelligence (ASI). AGI seeks to develop machines with generalized human intelligence, capable of sustaining long-term goals and intent and able to perform intellectual tasks that a human being can do.[16] Although this may be possible in the future, there are currently no signs of machines with self-sustaining long-term goals and intent, nor are they likely to be developed in the near future, according to the *Artificial Intelligence and Life in 2030* report.[17]

Sales and marketing professionals are not going to be replaced by robots or human-like machines anytime soon. In the short term, AI is an add-on feature to sales and marketing tech stacks to make our jobs more efficient and productive. It also assists big data analytics to help predictive and prescribed analytics.

Remember

Narrow AI (weak AI): Most of the mainstream AI-based tools focus on domain-dependent and problem-specific solutions. They are designed to perform specific tasks to accomplish short-term goals.

Artificial general intelligence (AGI, strong AI or human-like AI): Machines with generalized human intelligence, capable of sustaining long-term goals and intent, and performing intellectual tasks that a human being can do.

Although it's possible in the future, there are no present signs of machines with self-sustaining long-term goals and intent, nor are they likely to be developed in the near future, according to the *Artificial Intelligence and Life in 2030* report.

Balancing technology and human judgement

Technology has made our jobs easier, but does it also make us lazy? Rather than picking up a phone to wishing a good friend a 'happy birthday', we send a short text or a message via Facebook. Instead of pouring through the detailed reports generated by a dashboard, we choose to take recommendations presented by machines. With these layers upon layers of software, apps, and cloud services in the stacks, are we separating sales reps from customers and making it even harder to understand a buyer's needs? Are sales reps too dependent on tools and support groups like marketing or IT? Are sales reps getting lazy and soft? If sales reps are meeting their quotas, the concerns are probably overblown. If sales reps are not hitting their quotas, but the sales tech stack, sales processes and support teams are solid, an examination of where the problem lies is in order. It's important to recognize that technology is here to help us. Technology has the power to transform the different stages of sales processes and purchase journeys. But there's no substitute for 'elbow grease'– we still need to hustle to grow business.

A discussion of advances in computing technology is not complete without referencing Moore's Law. In 1965 Gordon Moore, co-founder of Intel, made a prediction that the number of transistors in a dense integrated circuit would double every year.[18] The chip industry has pretty much lived up to this prediction for several decades (it slowed to doubling every two years in 1975). This behaviour drove down the cost of processing power and spawned whole new industries empowered by cheap and powerful computing. The immense processing power coupled with massive amounts of data generated by end users also fostered AI development over the past several years.

As long as processing power continues to increase, technology will continue to evolve. As technology continues to evolve, we will need to continue to evaluate marketing and sales tech stacks. As we move further into the digital age, we need to recognize that technology is a double-edged sword. It can be a competitive advantage that helps bring a team together, but it can also derail the team by adding layers of bureaucratic complexities. To mitigate these risks, it's important to continually address and evaluate the sales stack and sales processes. It's not about keeping up with technologies or sourcing the next big and shiny object. It's about being mentally prepared to adopt new technologies or walk away from existing technologies whenever appropriate. Mark Godley, President of LeadGenius, stated that leading organizations should no longer look at their sales and marketing tech stacks in isolation, but as part of the 'revenue stack.' The integration of technology acts as the backbone for various departments to work together along the buyer's journey. It also provides the instrumentation to track and improve sales processes.

Bear in mind, when it comes to technology, it's a never-ending journey.

What you can do

1 Map your company's marketing and sales tech stacks.

2 Examine gaps in your tech stack and investigate tools or processes that can address those needs.

3 Identify how AI or big data analytics can assist your sales and lead generation processes.

Notes

1 Terminator Wiki. Skynet. http://terminator.wikia.com/wiki/Skynet

2 Scott Brinker. Marketing technology landscape supergraphic.
Chief Martech, 10 May 2017. https://chiefmartec.com/2017/05/
marketing-techniology-landscape-supergraphic-2017

3 Nicolas De Kouchkovsky. Sales tech landscape 2017: Making sense
of 700+ players. Sales Hacker. www.saleshacker.com/sales-
technology-landscape

4 Richard Potember. Perspectives on research in artificial intelligence
and artificial general intelligence relevant to DoD. https://fas.org/irp/
agency/dod/jason/ai-dod.pdf

5 Types of analytics: Descriptive, predictive, prescriptive analytics.
22 January 2018. www.dezyre.com/article/types-of-analytics-
descriptive-predictive-prescriptive-analytics/209

6 Mark Godley. Bah! Humbug! The Scrooge of B2B data wishes for a
better future. LinkedIn, 28 December 2017. www.linkedin.com/pulse/
bah-humbug-scrooge-b2b-data-wishes-better-future-mark-godley

7 Ibid.

8 Tom Hale. How much data does the world generate every minute?
26 July 2017. www.iflscience.com/technology/how-much-data-
does-the-world-generate-every-minute

9 Brett Grossfeld. A simple way to understand machine learning vs.
deep learning. 8 July 2017. www.zendesk.com/blog/machine-
learning-and-deep-learning

10 Everything you need to know about AI for CRM. www.salesforce.com/
form/pdf/ai-for-crm.jsp

11 Brett Grossfeld, op. cit.

12 LeadCrunch helps Odysses boost pipeline by 34%. https://drive.
google.com/file/d/0B2e_dLNb51agRDBBdVRqZ2lLNmM/view

13 Brad Power. How AI is streamlining marketing and sales.
Harvard Business Review, 12 June 2017. https://hbr.org/2017/06/
how-ai-is-streamlining-marketing-and-sales

14 Andrew Myers. Stanford's John McCarthy, seminal figure of artificial
intelligence, dies at 84. *Stanford News*, 25 October 2011. https://news.
stanford.edu/news/2011/october/john-mccarthy-obit-102511.html

15 Matthew Sparkes. Top scientists call for caution over artificial intelligence. *Telegraph*. 13 January 2015. www.telegraph.co.uk/technology/news/11342200/Top-scientists-call-for-caution-over-artificial-intelligence.html

16 AGI definition from AGI Society. www.agi-society.org

17 One hundred year study of artificial intelligence. Artificial intelligence and life in 2030. Stanford University. 2016. https://ai100.stanford.edu/sites/default/files/ai100report10032016fnl_singles.pdf

18 Tom Simonite. Moore's Law is dead. Now what? *MIT Technology Review*, 13 May 2016. www.technologyreview.com/s/601441/moores-law-is-dead-now-what/

Action.
Action.
Action.

The impediment to action advances action.
What stands in the way becomes the way.
MARCUS AURELIUS

Even though selling has been around for thousands of years, the different functions of an organization were not conceived until much later. After the Industrial Revolution, factories were established to manufacture products at scale and people were hired to do the work. Systems were needed to manage 'everything' in order for production to run smoothly. Specific corporate functions were created: human resource to handle employee records, hiring and firing; financial and accounting to track revenue, costs and payroll; purchasing to buy supplies and materials; marketing to promote products; and sales to sell products. Things before digital transformation were fairly straightforward: it was easy to define each department's roles and responsibilities and people knew the departments' boundaries.

The boundaries between functions begin to fade as technology continues to grow and expand to improve our efficiency and productivity by 'doing' our work, or integrating or merging different tasks and processes. In some cases, technology has been applied to integrating tasks from multiple departments, which creates disruption or confusion on roles and responsibilities among departments. For example: one role of sales enablement is to develop and deliver sales training. A sales enablement manager who is responsible for sales onboarding and training may develop a continuous training regimen, from a pre-onboarding curriculum and an onboarding bootcamp to a set of course work for the first three to six months, and then provide annual refreshers and updates. To accomplish this effectively it is necessary to integrate the company's email system (IT department), the employee performance system (HR department), the training platform (sales enablement department) and the content management library (marketing department). When salespeople complete the pre-onboarding curriculum, their managers will receive an email notification. After salespeople have taken tests for each subject in their curriculum, the score will be sent to their managers and automatically recorded in their HR records.

There's no longer a clear boundary between the sales enablement function and other departments. Sales enablement can belong to several departments. It is reasonable to decide that the sales enablement training methodology and platform should be scaled to company-wide onboarding efforts. The human resources department can easily argue that the training for sales enablement should be folded into their responsibilities to drive corporate efficiency. The sales team can argue that sales enablement has unique requirements and, therefore, the sales function should retain ownership of the entire effort. The marketing team can make the case that a big chunk of sales training content comes from the marketing team, therefore, it should be part of marketing (and even without this example, marketing often feel that sales belong in their area). Technology makes our job easier, but, along with evolving requirements and market conditions, it makes our roles and responsibilities murkier. With further integration, some roles and responsibilities can be consolidated, or even assigned to machines or AI. Organizational structures and roles and responsibilities will continue to morph as markets, customers, buying habits and technology evolve. This is a good thing. Close collaboration across many departments and redefined roles and responsibilities have to be addressed in order for companies to be successful.

There is an emerging fundamental change in the corporate landscape because of changing and blurring roles and responsibilities: some corporations are hiring fewer full-time employees and instead outsourcing a great deal of work to subcontractors and freelancers in HR, IT, manufacturing or even training. That trend alone will have unanticipated and unforeseen ramifications on corporate culture, communications flow, organizational structure, performance reviews, compensation, even the physical office planning and more. That does not mean that we should be passive and wait until the clouds clear to do something about it.

Remember

Because of the nebulous state of the sales enablement function, you can proactively propose what needs to be done to better enable the sales team. You are in control.

You can be the trailblazer that shapes your company's sales enablement activities. At the end of the day, sales enablement is about making the sales team efficient and effective so that they can close deals. Today, an increasing amount of sales organizations have adopted an account-based approach for handling customers through the buying cycles. This requires a team of sales, marketing, sales enablement and other functions to have a shared understanding of their firm's strategy, value propositions, sales tasks and corresponding selling behaviours. With technology as an enabler and a forcing function, these teams need to be more tightly integrated than ever before. You may step on each other's toes when the team are moving fast. That is OK as long as everyone is on the same page.

The following questions help you determine actionable steps that you can take:

- What can we change now?
- What can we improve?
- What can we add?

By the way, I am not forgetting about the 'why'. We should, by all means, examine the why behind what we do, what is requested and what we plan. But the why is simple: enable sales to close the deals. In this chapter we will go beyond 'why' and focus on 'what'. Before we do that, let's go back to my own definition of effective sales enablement from the earlier chapter:

> Deliver a positive customer experience by equipping sales with knowledge, skills, processes and tools through cross-functional collaboration in order to increase sales velocity and productivity.

Depending on your roles and responsibilities, you or your team are likely to be doing something covered by my definition. These questions will guide you to determine what actions you can take after finishing this book.

What can we change now?

Address immediate issues. Peter Drucker said it succinctly: 'Unless commitment is made, there are only promises and hopes... but no plans.'[1] The first step is to have a plan articulating how you will support your sales team.

Craft a simple one-pager to articulate your plans and actions to support the sales team. (See Figure 10.1.) Tie your tactics to sales and marketing objectives, starting with the company's business goals. Then, incorporate departmental objectives from your sales and marketing teams into your one-pager.

10.1

◯	BUSINESS GOALS			
☑	SALES OBJECTIVES			
☑	MARKETING OBJECTIVES			
↑+	SALES ENABLEMENT STRATEGY			
👤	INTERNAL SALES PERSONAS			
(X)	TARGET SALES ENABLEMENT IN COUNTRIES			
Q	LANGUAGES			
↑+	KEY TACTICS			
💡	KPIs			

Sales objectives are different from business goals. A company's goals might be defined in terms of revenue, gross profit, earnings before interest, tax, depreciation and amortization (EBITDA) targets, market segment share or new product growth percentage for the year. Sales objectives are what the sales team will do to accomplish the business goals. Marketing objectives are what the marketing team will do to help the sales team accomplish their goals. Many marketing teams have to focus on meeting corporate goals that many not be helping sales directly. For this one-pager, focus on the objectives that directly tie to sales.

Next, detail your sales enablement strategy by focusing on three to five initiatives that you will do to support sales as a marketer. You can also identify specific types of salespeople that you will support as 'internal sales team personas'. If you are supporting a global sales team and/or creating global content, you can also add country and language priorities as you see fit. Then, you can list the key tactics that you will use to support the overall sales enablement strategy.

The last element is key performance indicators (KPIs): three to five quantifiable metrics that you will measure and tie back to the overall sales goals. It's important to share proactively how you measure your own success and how these metrics tie back to the overall company goals.

If companies have not clearly defined their sales and marketing objectives, I'd recommend that you do so with urgency and review them with your sales and marketing management.

Remember

Identify the key tactics and actions that you will use, based on your roles and responsibilities, to support the sales team. With that one-pager, you can easily articulate how your contributions relate to the business goals, sales and marketing objectives.

This one-page document should be a guide for departments and individuals to develop their own plans. You can build on this one-pager by adding additional elements that are relevant to your department or group. For example: you can add the regions of sales teams that you will support. You can also specify the stages of the sales process that you will focus on. Add any elements required to make it clear to your internal stakeholders how you will be supporting and enabling them. It also serves as a plan of record on how you will support the sales team.

> **Remember**
>
> The one-pager needs to be done as early in the year as possible, to serve as a foundation and baseline to measure progress and success. It should be dynamic and revisited every quarter to identify what is working and what needs to be adjusted.

Documenting your plan is an easy way to help management understand your intended contributions at a specific point in time. It's important for a team or an individual contributor to be able to refer to this one-pager at any given time. As an individual contributor, you can use this information as a template to provide updates to your manager on a regular basis and ensure you are working on the right tasks and deliverables.

How can we improve?

Now that you have a plan, everyone is on board and plans are set in motion, what is next stage? Can you address departmental silos or better integration across tools? The question to ask is, 'How can we continually improve?' This can be addressed in two specific ways:

- how better to support our salespeople
- how better to support our customers

Supporting salespeople

This book details how better to support your sales teams from a marketer's point of view. I touched on the future trends that will impact salespeople and how marketing can help them. I shared my thoughts on marketing's role in sales enablement and how sales and marketing can better work together. I discussed how various marketing elements could be leveraged by sales efforts. I explained how brand and messaging apply to sales teams. I explored design, user experience and technology's role in sales enablement. I hope it provides ideas, and even a roadmap, on how better to support your sales team.

As a sales enablement person, it's important to evaluate your processes, team talent, and tools to determine how to improve. It does not mean that you need to take on additional work with your existing budget and resources. It means identifying opportunities and having a discussion with the management team to propose a plan with additional budget and resourcing to drive desired outcomes.

Supporting customers

For your customers, you should examine the current state of customer support and outbound marketing. Buyers deserve a clear, crisp, concise explanation of what we do and what we can do for them. They also need to know how we will do it, and how that's different from other vendors. Most importantly, they also need to know what we won't be able to do. We need to provide our customers with a user-friendly website with relevant content to help us gauge their interest through different stages of the sales funnel. If sales and marketing are working together on account-based initiatives and various marketing tactics are used, marketing needs to evaluate each method, review the results and optimize channels, and allocate budget as they see fit. I hear marketers complain that they are doing the same things every day. Even if it's the same email marketing, there are always opportunities to tweak content and strategies to improve relevance and response rates. It doesn't necessarily require a big budget and it doesn't have to be a big initiative. Just try something new. It's up to us to make it better even if we are using the same channels. Can we do AB testing a little better? Can we try to send out emails on a different day, time or cadence? Can we use customer-generated content? Can we change the contact fields on the landing page? Can we jazz up the appeal by using different copywriting, images or videos? That is the fun aspect of digital; you can easily make changes and try something new.

Curata CEO Pawan Deshpande shared an internal exercise that they did for mapping the customer journey.

He drew a line in the centre of the whiteboard and divided it into two big areas. (See Figure 10.2.) He listed customer touchpoints on the right side and all interactions by his company on the left side with arrows indicating the flow between each interaction and touchpoint. For example: a customer visiting the website requested a demo, which is listed on the right side. Then, on the left side, the list includes a demo enquiry email, which is sent to a member of the sales team, followed by an email sent back to the lead to schedule the demo with the assigned sales representative. In a similar manner, the whole process from initial interaction through sale is listed on the whiteboard.

This can foster a discussion between sales, marketing and even customer success teams to evaluate customers' journey and the handoffs between different team members. Pawan Deshpande uses this mapping process to identify what his team can do better to streamline the process. For example: when visitors click on 'request a demo', it will link to the marketing automation tool and activate an email notification to the sales team to contact the lead. In order to set a time for a demo with a prospect, a lot of back-and-forth emails and coordination were required which would often take days. Because of the back-and-forth communication, customers' desire waned, and only 40 per cent made it to the point of seeing a demo. With this exercise, the teams were able to identify the gap and address it with a solution that allows visitors to self-schedule the demo time at their convenience immediately from the website. This one change boosted the number of demos delivered from 40 per cent to 65 per cent, which had a significant downstream lift on their revenues.

It's about working together to review processes and workflows. Identify the gaps and find ways to improve. Process improvement and tool selections take time and effort. Even if you do it right, you don't usually see the impact for several months. Therefore, it can be hard to get people to commit over two or three quarters to execute

0.2

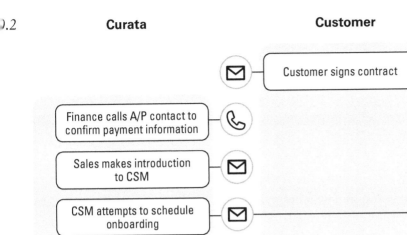

Curata   **Customer**

Customer signs contract

Finance calls A/P contact to confirm payment information

Sales makes introduction to CSM

CSM attempts to schedule onboarding

CSM provisions account and sends invite → Customer accepts invite

Customer schedules onboarding

CSM sends onboarding invite

CSM conducts initial onboarding — Customer attends initial onboarding

CSM sends onboarding follow-up

CSM schedules first QBR and sends invite

CSM marks subscription as launched

CSM requests confirmation for QBR — Customer confirms availability

CSM conducts next QBR — Customer attends QBR

CSM sends QBR follow-up notes

CSM sends invite for next QBR → Customer accepts invite

a long-term project, especially when marketing need to provide qualified leads and sales need to meet their quota every month and quarter. This is just additional work that everyone needs to do. I don't have an easy answer for this, except that senior management need to balance the trade-off between long term initiatives and short-term goals. You need to proactively address your workload with your manager.

What can we add?

Too often, the focus is exclusively on the short term and immediate goals. To foster long-term business growth, plans need to be put into action to address the long-term growth as well. While it's always good to search for easy wins, you should also make a holistic assessment of your overall sales efforts and what they need to stay with or ahead of your customers, the competition and the market. As an individual contributor, you can propose initiatives and ideas to the sales or marketing teams. It's difficult to take time out of the day-to-day grind to think strategically. But that is exactly what annual planning sessions are for. If your company has an annual planning process in which the next year's budget and priorities are discussed and set, I'd highly recommend using that event to think about a longer horizon as well and brainstorm initiatives that can position marketing to enable your company to excel.

When you are working on a plan for longer-term initiatives, you need to create a compelling case to convince key internal customers of the value of your proposition.

Remember

Build your case based on two key concepts: 'convince' and 'value'. Create a presentation to 'convince' management that your big ideas will aid both sales and marketing. You should also have information to showcase the monetary and non-monetary impacts and benefits.

Know the knowns

Lee Iacocca, former CEO of Chrysler Corporation in the 1980s, has a quote that really resonates with me: 'There is no substitute for accurate knowledge. Know yourself, know your business, know your men.'[2] Knowing yourself is about knowing what you can offer, what you can do and how you measure the success. Amy Pence at Alteryx and Diane Walker, ex-SAP sales enablement manager, love supporting sales. Amy knows what she can do to train sales. Diane makes sure her marketing programmes drive warm leads. Knowing your business is about knowing your company's overall direction, strategic imperatives and sales plans and then tying them together with a sales enablement strategy. Your understanding should be documented clearly on your one-pager. Knowing your 'men' may not be politically correct nowadays, but the essence of the quote is to know what makes your salespeople tick. I mentioned the option of creating a sales persona. It takes one to know one.

Salespeople can be cynical at times. You need to work hard to earn their respect and make sure they understand how you provide value. Otherwise, they will just ignore you. I have had my share of being ignored by my sales teams while launching tools and processes that were not adopted by the reps, even though some of the initiatives were requested by their leadership and I had their buy-in. One way or another, the projects were not successful. I didn't take it personally. I chose to learn from the failures and move on. Introspection and self-evaluation are required for continued future success.

Beware of the unknowns

Technology is rapidly changing how customers purchase, behave and communicate. When email was invented, no one foresaw phishing, spam and the other dark tricks that would pervade inboxes. When social media was launched, we thought it would connect everyone and make the world a better place. It did connect us, but whether or not it has made the world a better place is debatable. We just don't know how advancing martech and evolving technology stacks will impact sales enablement, collaboration and communications within various job functions. Beware of the unknowns, continually monitor trends and be ready to adopt and change.

Manage what you can change

In the corporate world, there are many internal and external issues that we cannot overcome as an individual or as a team. Some of the events that affect marketing and sales but are beyond our control include economic downturns, company politics, competitive landscape game changers, product launch delay due to manufacturing or sourcing issues, management changes, and even team goal misalignment. When you work on big initiatives, there will be times during which you feel as if you take one step forward and two steps backward. You will feel frustrated, angry and discouraged from time to time. That's part of the journey. That's part of life.

The question is what you can do to keep moving forward and turn setbacks into opportunities. To do that, you need to know what you can and cannot change. The key is to focus on what is in your control and plan around or mitigate issues caused by events you cannot control.

Actions advance actions

Essentially, a company's growth will hinge on the collaboration of sales and marketing departments, working together as one team with a common goal and focus on their customers. Even companies with the best alignment of sales and marketing can't stay productively aligned forever. Every strategy has an expiration date, because every business operates in an ever-changing environment. Make sure your marketing plan includes sales input and that your company's sales plans leverage marketing. Marketing is in many ways a company's hidden sales force, which has to engage and start working together productively with the sales team. Have a plan, address issues that come your way one by one and manage what you can change. The journey of one thousand miles is to start walking *now*. Steps advance steps. Actions advance actions. Just remember: when marketing is working seamlessly with its sales team, it creates a symbiotic relationship that is greater than the sum of its parts.

It's time to take action.

Notes

1 Peter Drucker. https://www.brainyquote.com/quotes/peter_drucker_121122?img=3 .

2 Lee Iacocca. https://www.brainyquote.com/quotes/lee_iacocca_120040

INDEX